In Time of Need

In Time of Need

The Meadville Lombard Reader
2005

Sermons and essays from the
Meadville Lombard Theological School community

Edited by
Tina Porter

Meadville Lombard Press
Chicago, Illinois

In Time of Need: The Meadville Lombard Reader 2005
Edited by Tina Porter
Copyright ©2006 by Meadville Lombard Theological School

First Edition 2006

Meadville Lombard Press
5701 S. Woodlawn Avenue
Chicago, IL 60637

Cover design and cover art by Marian Stewart

ISBN: 0-9702479-9-0
        978-0-9702479-9-5

Library of Congress Number: 2006927650

Printed in the United States of America

CONTENTS

FOREWORD

In Time of Need.

That is the title of the sermon the Rev. Matt Tittle delivered to his Unitarian Universalist congregation in Houston, Texas on the Sunday following his return from the Gulf Coast of Louisiana. While there, he assisted with the clean-up following the devastation of Hurricane Katrina. And, while there, he witnessed the full range of human response: deepest suffering and heroic courage, passive apathy and engaged compassion, mere survival and great spiritual uplift. That Sunday also happened to be the fourth anniversary of the day box cutters and airplanes were transformed into weapons used against the citizens of the United States of America.

The whole world is caught in a time of need. Globally, the repercussions of the terrorist attacks of September 11 continue to shape our era. That the United States is carrying out a war in Iraq that is predicated on dubious moral and political grounds is but one example. Domestically, when the roof of the Superdome was peeled back by Katrina's force, it exposed the degree to which we fail those who most need the embrace of our human capacity for compassion and justice: the poor, the infirm, the children, and the elderly.

It is a time of need in every precinct of the world, a time that begs for a liberal religious response. For in our Unitarian Universalist perspective, there is to be found renewed hope and imaginative solutions.

That is apparent in this collection of sermons and essays written by members of the wider Meadville Lombard Theological School community. These authors and preachers—students, professors, and alumni/ae alike—provide us with a way to begin looking at how we Unitarian Universalists might lead our battered humanity away from violence and adversity and hatred toward the holy shores of peace and plenty and love.

These sermons and essays demonstrate that we are specially suited to do this:

Matt Tittle, MDiv '04, seeks solace from the chaos brought on by Katrina in the stories of the Hebrew and Christian traditions. Out of those stores he finds delivery from his personal anguish and challenges America to grow beyond our fears.

John Cullinan, a third-year Meadville Lombard Master of Divinity student, calls on his personal experience as a student chaplain who served that capacity with two fundamentalist theological students—one Muslim and one Christian—to urge us to stretch theology to its most practical dimension, the dimension of action.

"Out from Walden" was preached by Patrick O'Neill, DMin '79, at the Service of the Living Tradition at the Unitarian Universalist Association's General Assembly in 2005. It was the perfect venue for Patrick to challenge our newly-ordained ministers to embrace the full tradition of Unitarian Universalism, to serve not only our pietistic heritage, but our prophetic heritage, too. "[W]e hold dear the precious legacy handed down to us," he says so powerfully, "so we recognize that we exist as churches, as Free-faith communities, and as those ordained to work in the name of this legacy, we recognize that we exist to serve and to make better the tenor of our times, to give meaning to our days."

In "The Very Hardest Thing," Edward Frost, DMin '74, tells us that it is possible to recognize truth and hold faith at the very same time. "I believe that it is the task of the Unitarian Universalist minister," he says, "to do the very hardest thing—to proclaim and maintain a faith, while struggling with the truths that, without a faith to live by, would hollow us out and beat us down."

In "Long Come the Millennium," Mark Ward, MDiv '04, looks at the Book of Revelations to weave a sermon that reminds us of the importance of our Unitarian Universalism. "It is critical that as we work to organize a response in support of our life-affirming faith, one that sees salvation as the work for wholeness and reconciliation of all human-kind," he writes, "we also stay true to our principles and our own humanity."

And Valerie Mapstone Ackerman, MDiv '98, in her essay, "How to Name Your Farm," writes about a vanished dog and the imprint that dog left on her, her life, her farm. There is reverence in this piece of writing. It connects us to the world—and the life—that is to be cherished and saved in this time of need.

These authors, and the others whose words appear in this book, call on themes that Unitarian Universalists perk up to spontaneously: the saving nature of communities that are theologically and culturally inclusive, the link between the spiritual life and the life of service, the faith that we human beings can shape our world to the better and to the best. These are also the themes out of which Unitarian Universalist ministers are prepared at Meadville Lombard Theological School.

As it happens, I know personally each contributor to this book. It gives me great pleasure now to introduce them to the wider readership of this collection. I know you will agree with me that their presence in the world provides great comfort. These are Unitarian Universalist men and women who are guiding the world toward its greatest fulfillment. Meadville Lombard Theological School takes pride in having played a role in their development.

Although this is a time of need, it is also a time of promise.

Lee Barker, DMin '78 DD '01
President
Meadville Lombard Theological School
Chicago, Illinois
April 21, 2006

Editor's Note

In Time of Need is the first of what we hope will be many installments of an annual Reader of sermons, essays and papers written by members of the Meadville Lombard community.

In October 2005, the call went out to those members of our community for whom we had e-mail addresses on hand, seeking their contributions to this first-ever publication. The response to this admittedly incomplete call made it clear there is a wealth of wisdom in our community and we had struck on an idea long overdue—collecting that wisdom and making it available to the public.

We could not include all the pieces submitted to us and paring it down to the selections you find in this volume was no easy task. But there came a point when the selections you find here seemed to make sense together, painting a cohesive picture of the problems the people of the world are facing now. But there also was a sense, in each of these pieces, of the overwhelming need to embrace hope in times of collective tragedy or personal despair, and of the hope that can be found in the Unitarian Universalist faith.

We look forward to continuing this new tradition, of collecting the works of those thoughtful and inspirational leaders within our faith movement.

Sincerely,

Tina Porter
Director of Communications
Meadville Lombard Theological School
April 21, 2006

In Time of Need

Matt Tittle, MDiv '04

Bay Area Unitarian Universalist Church

Houston, TX

September 2005

Reading: Medieval Jewish Story

A rabbi spoke with God about heaven and hell. "I will show you hell," God said, and they went into a room which had a large pot of stew in the middle. The smell was delicious, but around the pot sat people who were famished and desperate. All were holding spoons with very long handles which reached to the pot, but because the handles of the spoons were longer than their arms, it was impossible to get the stew back into their mouths. "Now I will show you heaven," God said, and they went into an identical room. There was a similar pot of stew, and the people had identical spoons, but they were well nourished and happy. "It's simple," God said, "You see, they have learned to feed one another." (Buehrens, p. 119)

Nothing will ever be the same in this country, and for that I am both grieving deeply and am incredibly grateful.

In the Christian scriptures, Jesus opens his Sermon on the Mount with a prayer, the Beatitudes. This was near the beginning of his ministry, but his reputation had begun to spread and many followed him to hear this sermon. He climbed the hill, turned to the people and commenced to change the world. It is no wonder that this radical, itinerant preacher from Nazareth was eventually prosecuted and crucified. His message of love, hope, and inner faith—that the lower classes, the meek, the persecuted, and the peaceful people of the world were truly those who would inherit the joy and wonder of all creation—was too dangerous a message for the authorities. He told the oppressed masses that they were the ones who were truly blessed, that they were the salt of the earth and the light of the world. He told them repeatedly that their own faith and their inner strength would save them from all the suffering the world could heap upon them.

Last week, five of us from the Bay Area Unitarian Universalist Church, four others from the Northwoods Unitarian Universalist Church, three from First Unitarian Universalist Church, and a guy named Mike from Madison, Wisconsin, were at the North Shore Unitarian Universalist Church in LaCombe, Louisiana. We helped Rev. David Ord secure the roof, which had been torn off by Hurricane Katrina, and we helped clear the property of fallen trees. Mostly, I think we provided David with much needed spiritual support and fellowship. Most of his congregation has left the area because they are jobless and homeless.

At the worship service last Sunday morning, attended mostly by our work crews, David told us the story from the gospels of Matthew, Mark, and Luke in which Jesus calms a storm during a boat trip on a lake, probably the Sea of Galilee. Jesus falls asleep and the storm comes. The boat is rocking side-to-side, being swamped; meaning seawater is coming up onto the deck from the port and starboard sides. The boat is wallowing in the sea, which could cause it to capsize. The disciples wake Jesus. They are in great distress, don't know what to do, and implore him to calm the storm. Now, in Mark's recounting of this story it says Jesus is sitting at the back of the boat on a cushion. Although it doesn't specifically say so, this would mean he is tending the rudder. But he falls asleep and perhaps the boat moves parallel rather than perpendicular to the waves, which is a dangerous position in a storm. You always steer into the waves, never getting stuck in the trough between swells. Jesus fell asleep at the wheel, if you will. When he woke up, he calmed the storm and then said to the disciples, "Where is your faith?"

You see, the disciples could have taken hold of the tiller themselves and steered the boat to a safe course, even in the midst of the storm, but they were lost and stifled. When they woke Jesus, they said to him, "Teacher, do you not care that we are perishing?" Jesus bailed them out, but again appealed, as he always did, to their inner spirit and ability—to their faith—to their trust.

Friends, we are lost. It is time again to have faith that we, all of us together, can and will change the world. Neither Jesus nor any of the other historical or modern day prophets are going to the mountaintop to tell us what to do. Jesus isn't going to bail us out of this storm, but we need to heed his words. We need to start feeding each other with our long spoons.

The most powerful country on the globe has been brought to its knees. Not by a hurricane. Not by the terrorist attacks on New York and Washington, DC, four years ago today, but by our own failure in the past 229 years to attend to our greatest weakness—the social, economic, and racial inequities that that have plagued our nation since its founding. Our country, as great as it may be, as free as we may want to think we are, was established via the conquest of indigenous peoples, flourished through imported human slave labor, and thus was founded upon a resulting culture of pervasive racism and economic division of the classes.

Nearly 100 years after our Declaration of Independence, slavery was abolished, but only after a horrific civil war. Nevertheless, racism and classism remained strong in the United States of America. It took another 100 years, in the 1960s when the Civil Rights Act was passed, to guarantee some semblance of legal rights for all citizens, regardless of race. Even today, our nation remains segregated and unequal along racial and economic lines. Hurricane Katrina did not create this disaster. This hurricane was the most anticipated and studied potential natural disaster in our times. Hurricane Katrina was simply a catalyst. A wake up call if you will, like the attacks of September 11, that something is terribly wrong and needs to change.

We have spent the past 229 years sitting around a delicious pot of stew. We can smell the rich aroma of diversity, of love, of compassion, and of fellowship in that stew. But we keep our spoons to ourselves because they are ours. We have been living all this time in hell, famished and desperate because we have not been feeding each other.

I don't blame any individual for what happened this week. I don't use the terms racism and classism lightly. What we are experiencing is the result of at least hundreds of years of institutional inequality and oppression that have become so much a part of our culture that we are blind to it. No one is blind right now. We are all wide awake. Our eyes are wide open, and we can see the very real effects of a nasty heritage that we never bothered to correct. We have that opportunity now. You and I didn't cause this, but we can reverse it. Tens of thousands of people weren't trapped in New Orleans when the storm came because you and I wanted them to be trapped. But we can now reverse the underlying problem by staying awake and transforming ourselves one by one, each of us and all of us, until the world is a different place.

I need to tell some stories. Six years ago when my father died, in the weeks that followed I was so affected by the experience of caring for him and then losing him, that I remember actually being more alive and present in my interactions with others. I experienced great joy every time I interacted with another person, whether it was a loved one or complete stranger. I couldn't help but look them in the eye, and greet them, thank them and smile with them. For several weeks, I had this hyper-awareness to the presence and worth of others and my interdependence with them. My dad's death was the catalyst that prompted me to radically change my life. I decided to become a minister.

Last week, I was trying by phone to help get a family out of the Astrodome and onto a Greyhound bus to Atlanta, Georgia where a job waited for them. When it came time to get them to the bus station, I could not leave Clear Lake and so asked a colleague if he could help. He went to find the family and get them to the station. When leaving the Astrodome he said it took over an hour just to get the Metrorail line on foot because he was wearing his clerical collar and was stopped constantly by people seeking prayer. He even heard four confessions!

What struck me though, is that he said he did not see a single refugee nor did he see a single evacuee. He said he saw thousands of sisters and brothers. That is where we are now folks. All the barriers are down and we have the opportunity to embrace each other in this country in a way that we never have before.

Just two days ago, I attended a meeting of Christian ministers here in the Bay Area, at which I was a bit of a novelty, and was given a special welcome. I was the only non-Christian. I was the other. But the barriers were down and we held hands, prayed, read scripture, and talked about how we could come together in the face of this unimaginable and seemingly insurmountable tragedy.

This horrible tragedy is an opportunity, a moment of grace, a chance that may not come again for a generation or more to change the very fabric of our young nation. I'll let that settle in for a minute.

We have the opportunity to end the racial and economic inequality in our culture. We will be at fault if we don't seize this opportunity. I want this country to be a different place before I'm gone. When I said this at a UU ministers' meeting this week, one of my colleagues said, "I hope you're right. I hope that things will change, but I'm afraid that they won't." No, things won't change unless we decide to change them. Nothing will change unless each one of us decides to be transformed by this experience. I really don't think we have a choice, but we have a chance.

All of you have been heroic these past two weeks. You've been volunteering your time and money and compassion in amazing ways in response to the immediate needs of this disaster.

> *Blessed are those who hunger and thirst for righteousness, for*
> *they will be filled.*
> *Blessed are the merciful, for they will receive mercy.*
> *Blessed are the pure in heart, for they will see God.*
> *Blessed are the peacemakers, for they will be called the children*
> *of God. (Mt. 5:13-12, NRSV)*

We have just begun, friends. The status quo has changed and your mercy, your purity, your peacemaking are now the norm. There is no turning back. Anyone who has done a significant amount of service in his or her life, whether volunteer or paid, whether within your own community or around the world, will tell you that it is simply and unavoidably transforming. It will change your life, and therefore will change the life of every person you encounter. Please don't help a single person. As long as you are simply helping, the boundaries of them and us are still securely in place. There are no helpers and there is no one who needs your help any more than you need theirs. There are only thousands, millions, of sisters and brothers.

This is a great time of need. I know the task at hand is overwhelming and it will be easy for us to get lost on this path. Most of you have already experienced feelings of despair and hopelessness with your efforts because no matter what you do it is not enough. You've had some sleepless nights. Most of us, me included, have felt guilty that we are not doing enough. There are not enough hours in the day. These feelings are natural, but don't buy into them for one minute. Don't shortchange yourselves. You are changing the world. Nothing more, nothing less. Whether you have thrown $5 into the collection plate, a can of beans into a basket, or have spent every waking hour in one of the shelters, you are changing everything.

Four years ago, a generation of young Americans was without a defining historical moment in their lives. Now they have two. They will never forget the attacks of September 11, 2001 and will never forget the unnecessary aftermath of Hurricane Katrina. We need to break through the fear and break down the barriers that keep us from understanding why people would fly airplanes into skyscrapers and why thousands of people would simply be left out of the planned evacuation of a major city. We are a young nation, but are growing up fast. We do not have a choice but to change. We simply don't have a choice.

Take hold of the rudder, friends, and we will calm the storm. Liberate yourselves from hell on earth and change it into heaven by feeding someone else with your long spoon and, more importantly, by allowing them to feed you. This is the defining moment of our generation. Americans have never known life without deep inequalities. I am ready to devote the rest of my life to ensuring that these divisions are melted away. I hope you will join me. We have a long journey ahead of us. Bless each and every one of you for what you are doing.

Amen

How We Walk Together

John A. Cullinan

Ministerial Intern

Unity Temple UU Congregation

Oak Park, IL

October 2005

"So, how do you Unitarians use the Bible, anyway?"

I had been expecting this question. From the moment I had begun my work as an intern chaplain at the hospital, I knew that at some point I was going to be getting into a debate, or even an argument, about religious belief and authority. With such a broad range of religious cultures and beliefs working together in a relatively small space, the theological infighting was, I believed, inevitable. So, when Michael, the fundamentalist evangelical in the office, asked me the Bible question, I came back with my prepared response.

"It's one book out of many that we use. It's a source of inspiration, and it's open to interpretation, but it's not in any way authoritative. Some of us don't use it at all," I said, then steeled myself. I went into an intellectually defensive stance, and waited with my breath held for the ideological pummeling I was certain would follow.

Michael paused for a moment and thought about what I had just said. "Oh," he replied, "I guess that cancels out the next question I was going to ask. Never mind, then." And then he turned back to his computer to continue writing up a report on one of his patient visits from earlier that morning.

And I stood there, stunned.

Where was the fight, the attempt to argue against my scriptural flippancy and win my soul for Jesus? Where was the theological debate I'd been expecting?

The answer to these questions was deceptively simple, and had been staring me in the face for weeks before this exchange with my evangelical co-worker.

On most of the shifts I worked at the hospital, the intern chaplains' suite was usually occupied by three people: myself (the liberal Unitarian Universalist); Michael, the afore-mentioned conservative-evangelical-fundamentalist Christian; and Wajid, a rare specimen, the oft-talked-about-but-seldom-seen-up-close-fundamentalist Muslim.

You might expect dangerous chemical reactions to occur between such disparate, volatile elements when placed in the crucible of a shared office. Your expectations, like mine, would be confounded.

Michael and Wajid's tenures at the hospital had preceded mine by a few months, and they were already fast friends by the time I arrived on the scene. Their camaraderie perplexed many who knew them and their religious backgrounds. At best, folks in the hospital expected of each a grudging tolerance of the other; what they got instead was a close working friendship between the two. Other chaplains scrambled for explanations for a relationship that seemed to them impossible.

"It's their fundamentalism," one said to me. "It gives them a shared worldview." On the surface, that seemed like a reasonable explanation. But the sources of each of their "fundamentals" came from such different worlds, it seemed improbable to me that a shared love for literal interpretation of their respective scriptures was enough to form such a strong bond between the two. Coupled with this doubt was the fact that, the more I worked with the two, the more I became drawn into the circle of this working relationship. Fundamentalism certainly was not the factor that connected me to them.

What was it, then?

After the Bible-fight-that-never-happened between Michael and myself, we went back to our respective report writing. When a few moments had passed, he sat down beside me.

"I've got a patient you need to go visit. I think he needs a different face besides mine."

"When you're done there," said Wajid, "I need to get both of your perspectives on one of my visits."

And there was my answer.

None of us had come into the hospital to debate theology. We had come to the hospital to "do" theology. We had come to the hospital with a sense of mission and ministry, and our shared sense of mission, our drive to meet the needs of others—our practical theology—had trumped our conceptual, ideological theologies.

Here is one of my favorite jokes about Unitarian Universalists: wherever two or more are gathered, no one will agree and coffee will be served.

Here is one of my favorite questions from the Hebrew Scriptures: the prophet Amos asks, "Can two people walk together unless they are agreed?"

The Unitarian Universalist Association's Commission on Appraisal begins its latest study, *Engaging Our Theological Diversity*, by asking an important question: "Where is the unity in our theological diversity?"

There is a certain tension in that question that feels something like the rift that opens in the pairing of the Unitarian joke and the quote from Amos. It is a tension that has been building up since the time of the merger of Unitarianism and Universalism in 1961. Two religions with distinct theological centers join together, but avoid staking any claim on theological ground—perhaps in keeping with both churches traditions' of non-creedalism, or perhaps out of some fear that the theologies might not be at all compatible. The benefit of this circumstance is the creation of a "big tent" sense of inclusiveness when it comes to religious belief. The drawback is that, once you're inside the tent, you sit at a table with those who seem to share your belief, and rarely interact with the other tables—at least when it comes to beliefs. This often translates into a certainty that, on some level, we are being excluded from full participation.

In Unitarian Universalism today, there is—more often than not—a fear or mistrust of the theology of "the other." That sense of exclusion leads many to believe that they are somehow in a minority. This fear shows itself most sharply when leaders in the church begin throwing around phrases and ideas such as "a language of reverence" or "unity in theological diversity."

After the Commission on Appraisal presented their report at General Assembly in June, 2005, I began to hear remarkably similar comments from Unitarian Universalists who identified themselves along all points of the theological spectrum.

"That language won't be my language."

"They're not talking about me."

And, most disheartening: "They're trying to take my religion away from me."

The overwhelming sense people gave me at General Assembly was that, whatever is happening to Unitarian Universalism—and something is happening—it isn't going to include them.

On the converse side of the feeling that everything would be lost theologically, was the notion that, for some reason, one's "side" needed to have some sort of outright win. Coupled with the desperation felt over the lack of inclusion was a seeming urge to play theology as some sort of zero-sum, winner-take-all game. In one on-line discussion group, the conversation around the idea of unity in diversity became framed around a question of "tipping points."

"What are the circumstances," it was asked, "in which you would feel you no longer belong in your own religious home?" It is discussions such as this that lead one of my colleagues to refer to the unity question as, "The great denominational red herring." It's a good question on the surface, but one that ultimately leads to griping and negativity, and not any sort of constructive discussion about the question of our unity. A sense of fear becomes evident in the discussion, and much of that fear centers on the use of words.

This is hardly surprising. We are a denomination in love with words. After all, the high point of a majority of Unitarian Universalist worship services is when some guy or gal in a nice suit (or maybe even a robe) stands up in the pulpit and talks at you for fifteen to twenty minutes.

But, are words sufficient for faith? When we talk about a language of reverence, what do we mean when we say "language?" When we talk about finding unity in diversity, are we merely focusing on the words of personal beliefs and creeds?

I believe that language, specifically a spiritual language, inhabits many more dimensions than just mere words. My attempts to communicate with you on a spiritual level begin with ideas rooted in personal experience. Sometimes these ideas are verbal in nature. Often times they are not. I translate these ideas into the spoken word, and release those words from the pulpit or in a pastoral conversation, knowing full well that the words I speak and the words you hear are two entirely different creatures. Ideally, my words translate back into ideas in your minds.

What are the odds that our ideas look the same at the end of this process?

Now, perhaps by conspiracy of time and culture we might share some common, archetypal ideas or experiences that help to bridge the gap between our ideas and our words. The more concrete the word or experience, the easier it is to build that bridge.

If I say the word "brown," the majority of you are probably thinking the same thing.

If I say the word "dance," some groups of different images are starting to crop up here and there, perhaps divided along generational lines.

And what if I were to say the word "grace?"

Or "salvation?"

Or even "God?"

Do these words do my ideas justice? Are my ideas and your ideas remotely connected?

Are we even speaking the same language?

If mere words are insufficient, then, what's left?

I used to keep a post-it note near my computer when I was writing my entrance essay for seminary. It read, "Faith is a verb."

Or, in the words of my undergraduate acting professors: "Show. Don't tell."

The church requires more than our words. It demands an active, practical element to faith. The action—the mission—becomes the third dimension of this religious vocabulary, and our faith becomes something demonstrable rather than something merely debatable.

It is interesting to note that the Arabic word for belief comes from a root that means "that which can be shown."

I learned that from a Muslim.

Wajid, Michael, and I continued working out of our shared office for most of the summer months. As we worked together in our shared ministry, our appreciation for one another's faiths deepened. Granted, we avoided volatile topics such as scripture and interpretation, but what we learned through the daily exercise of our practical theologies was what it was about our faiths that impelled us into this ministry. What we would not have been able to understand had we merely been sitting in a room *talking about* our religions, we were able to embrace about each other because we had *ministered together* first.

When it came time for Michael and Wajid to move on, the chaplaincy staff sat down together to worship and wish them well. The two friends led the service, each bringing a piece of their own faith traditions into the chapel. Michael read from the Bible, and for a moment I was able to see what he saw in scripture through the filter of his ministry. More amazing was Wajid, who opened the service with the traditional call to prayer in Arabic. It is a language I do not speak, although I am aware of the English translation of the call. To see Wajid in that moment through the lens of our shared understanding of our call to service was to see an oft-misunderstood religion breach barriers of culture and language for one brief moment and become something beautiful.

Disparate faiths brought us together. The call to comfort the sick and the dying and their loved ones opened our faiths up to each other. We left with our faiths enriched by the shared mission.

I was concerned that perhaps this understanding I had gained of the place of mission in religious dialogue came out of a special circumstance. Perhaps it was possible that Michael, Wajid, and I had achieved something special at one time, in one place, with results not repeatable outside the zone of the hospital.

My first week as Intern Minister in Oak Park proved this fear unfounded. Within a week of arriving at Unity Temple, I found myself sitting in a room of clergy and other representatives from multiple faiths: Christians (both liberal and conservative), Jews, Buddhists, and more. We had come together to discuss how we could better coordinate our efforts in serving the needs of the poor and homeless in the community. The only audible religious language was the prayer that opened the brunch. After that, the clergy got down to business, sharing stories of what they knew of the needs in the community, and building a plan to create a central place of service where local churches can channel their resources so that all needy members of the community can find a way back into society. The word "God" was never spoken. But you'd better believe the language was one of faith.

Our varied faiths brought us to the table, but the work kept us there.

The exercise of a practical theology is by no means an ultimate solution. The mission is not a replacement for honest theological dialogue.

The "big tent" of Unitarian Universalism holds many different traditions. Some people cherish their heritage; others are wounded by it. There is talking that needs to be done, but sometimes the words get in the way. Sometimes we are left stranded at the table with those "just like us," afraid to engage with others for fear of being labeled "different." Or, worse, discovering there is no place for us in the tent after all. But, where do we start when words are not enough?

Do we, like the builders of Babel, abandon the job when our language is confused? Do we echo Amos, and ask if we can possibly walk together without being in agreement?

Or do we, perhaps, name our purpose and our mission in the world, put words aside for a while, and just begin to walk?

Religion, Terrorism, and the End of the Nation State

David E. Bumbaugh, BD '64

Professor of Ministry

Oxford Round Table

Lincoln College

Oxford University

August 2005

Several months ago, at the southern end of Lake Michigan, in the city of Chicago, the Virgin Mary made a miraculous appearance. In a shadowed tunnel that carries vehicular and pedestrian traffic under a busy major motorway, a dark stain emerged on one wall. Someone, passing by, determined that this stain, in fact, was an image of the Virgin.

Word began to spread. The faithful and the curious came in increasing numbers to see for themselves. Soon the damp, dark, tunnel—filled with noxious fumes from passing traffic—had become a focus of pilgrimage as hundreds of people gathered to pay homage before this miraculous event, placing candles and flowers in adoration at the base of the stain.

Fearful of the consequences for a crowd of people gathered in a poorly-lighted area where vehicular traffic flowed constantly, the city dispatched maintenance people to investigate. After examining the wall, the city workers reported that the image on the wall had been caused by the seepage of salt water from the expressway overhead. They explained to the press and to all who would listen that during the winter, in order to keep traffic flowing, the city salted major thoroughfares whenever snow or ice threatened. Over time, the runoff from that effort, seeping through the walls of the tunnel, had created the dark stain.

The explanation made great sense. With quiet reason, it explained everything. It didn't matter in the least to the faithful who insisted that there, on the wall of that grimy underpass, the Virgin had decided to appear to the citizens of Chicago. What did it matter if the vehicle she chose was salt-water run-off? And by the hundreds, they continued to come to pay homage and to worship the Virgin in this most unlikely of grottos.

This impromptu center of religious devotion is only the most recent in a series of phenomena that suggest that faith is alive and well in the heart of the secular city. In an urban setting the size of Chicago, tragedies, large and small, are a regular part of life. Children are struck by automobiles. A porch collapses, carrying partygoers to sudden death. Old people and young die in house fires. Sometimes a bystander is the unintended victim of a shooting. The newspapers duly report these random events and often the report is accompanied by a photograph of the impromptu altars that spring up at the sites of such tragedies. On the public street, near where an automobile accident or a shooting ended a life, or near the site of a fatal house fire small bouquets of flowers appear, sometimes some candles, sometimes teddy-bears and dolls, and often scraps of paper containing handwritten prayers or snatches of poetry. Responding to some persistent innate urge that is older than organized religion, nameless, faceless individuals attempt to endow a senseless tragedy with some larger meaning by marking the spot, bestowing upon it a greater, albeit temporary, significance.

This behavior is not confined to the city of Chicago. Throughout the western world, there seems to be a religious need that is no longer met within the many churches of Christendom—a religious need that no longer finds adequate expression within the carefully-defined and well-maintained structures of organized religion; a religious need that finds those conventional structures too confining and, like a dammed up torrent, sometimes breaks through the barriers of convention and floods out, carving new channels of expression.

I would call your attention to the phenomenon in recent decades by which popular culture has created a number of secular saints, whose deaths have evoked a deluge of grief and who, in the common perception, have attained a superhuman stature. Consider the outpouring of grief at the death of John Lennon or Princes Diana, or the near-messianic stature attained by Bob Marley and Elvis Presley. Gifted and talented and beautiful people though they may have been, the response to their deaths has been all out of proportion to the accomplishments of their lives. They have been elevated to the role of secular saint—their lives endowed with lofty and unchallengeable significance.

Or consider the response by the secular world to the deaths of such religious figures as Mother Theresa or Pope John Paul II. People who have little or no involvement with organized religion, and who have little real knowledge or understanding of the accomplishments of these contemporary icons have, by the millions, offered tribute and homage to their lives and their importance. This phenomenon tells us less about the lives of those so honored than it does about the unmet spiritual needs of millions of contemporary women and men.

All of this is occurring at a time when, throughout the western world, it is clear that organized religion is in a state of serious decline. While millions gathered to pay tribute to the late Pope, the churches and Cathedrals of much of Europe stood virtually empty. Indeed, it was said of Pope John Paul II that he could draw people to the public square, but not to the pews. In the United States, said to be the most religious of the western nations, mainline religious bodies—Catholic and Protestant—have struggled with declining numbers for decades and nothing seems to stop, or even slow, the steady weakening of the great religious bodies that once dominated the cultural life of the nation. Study after study reveals the contradictory statistics that suggest the American people are still deeply concerned about matters of faith, while fewer and fewer of them connect that faith to institutional forms of religion. Increasingly, Americans define themselves as spiritual, but not religious. This is another way of saying that they worship at the impromptu altars of their own devising, rather than at those of the institutional churches.

Religious institutions that seem to be prospering in the United States, and perhaps elsewhere, are those that eschew denominational ties and traditional loyalties, that reject clear theological definition, that are ostentatious in discarding forms, garbs and structures that have a religious look to them.

In buildings that look like commercial establishments, offering a mixture of what has been called "theology light" messages—aimed at delivering a potpourri of self-help advice and unchallenged and unchallenging spirituality—and upbeat contemporary music, they blur the line between religion and entertainment and gather people by the thousands. To what purpose and to what end, and in response to what ultimate vision, no one seems to know.

A recent study of the religious impulse in Great Britain concludes that much of the spiritual life of the people has moved out of the churches and into what is vaguely identified as new-age religious alternatives. The study concludes that the emptying out of the institutional church will result in less than three percent of the population having any affiliation with or involvement in traditional congregational life.

Clearly, something of major importance is happening in the religious life of the western world. Whether we define religion as a structure of shared beliefs concerning the nature and meaning of existence, or as a pattern of ritual responses to the cycles of life and the exigencies that often interrupt them, or as a system by which communities exist through time, define themselves and mark their boundaries, it seems obvious that the religious life of the west is moving outside its churches and is challenging formal religion with an amorphous spirituality. Christendom has crumbled away and in its place is a new thing, difficult to define precisely because it has yet to coalesce into a recognizable form.

This shift in religious loyalties and religious expression is part of a larger, global shift that has been underway for the past half century or more—a global shift that has deep and profound implications for all the major institutions that have seemed so permanent and beyond challenge that we have failed to understand that we may be living in one of those moments in time when history becomes discontinuous, when the old is swept away and a new world order is created.

Ten years ago, I had occasion to make a visit to Eastern Europe. We flew from New York to Budapest. As we walked into the air terminal in that ancient city, I was suddenly aware of a familiar face on the television monitors. There, in the heart of Central Europe, I was welcomed by the American situation comedy, *The Golden Girls*, dubbed into Hungarian. Walking the streets of Budapest, I was invited to have lunch at the Colonel's Kentucky Fried Chicken, or at Burger King, or at the most elegant McDonalds I have ever seen. Young people walked the streets in the global costume of teen-agers: blue jeans and tee-shirts emblazoned with the logo of the Hard-Rock Cafe.

Later in that visit I had occasion to spend some time in Romania's province of Transylvania. I remember one small, isolated village: no paved streets, served by a single road so potholed and rutted that to drive on it was to risk permanent damage to any motor vehicle, and a telephone service that for some reason only functioned for a few hours each afternoon. In any kind of emergency, particularly at night, assistance would be a long time coming to that community.

But in the middle of this isolated village, on the roof of a sturdy house, one could see a satellite dish. And at the appropriate time, the village gathered to watch reruns of the American television melodrama, *Dallas*. And throughout the village I encountered young people who had learned to speak English by listening to American television.

This experience symbolizes what is happening across much of our planet, as ancient indigenous cultures are invaded and eroded, if not swept away by an irresistible wave of western technology and the value systems embedded within that technology. Biologists tell us we are living through an era in which we are witnessing a massive die-off of species. What may be less obvious, but perhaps just as true, is that we are living in an era defined by a massive die off of indigenous cultures. We call it progress, and perhaps it is, but it is accompanied by a soul-wrenching shift in values and perspectives. It should come as no surprise that in many places traditional peoples feel themselves under unremitting attack from an outside power that inevitably commodifies their culture, their traditions, their way of life, killing the soul and transforming all into a global system that produces profit for someone else.

Nor should it surprise us that this vast upheaval in the human experience should have profound consequences for political systems across the planet. Several trends seem to be occurring simultaneously, but all of them function to weaken the system of nation states that has characterized much of the world since the onset of modernity. Assaulted by the acids of modernity, many peoples attempt to defend and preserve life styles and values by escape into cultural enclaves, in the process withdrawing their loyalties from the nation and defining themselves in terms of an ethnicity often more the result of creative construction than historic reality, or a religious identity built of convenient shreds and pieces of a once great and now only vaguely understood heritage. As these groups engage in status struggles within the larger body politic, it often appears that the unity of the nation is at risk.

In this context, the nation state has lost much of its traditional power. With the emergence of globalization, and the awareness of the inescapable consequences of a planetary civilization, the nation state has lost a number of its monopolies. It has lost its ability to regulate its economic life; it has lost control of its borders; it has lost its ability to regulate the flow of information; it has lost its monopoly on force and terror. It has become the focus of global conflicts between sects and ethnic groups which, in an earlier age, scarcely knew of each other's existence.

The most powerful nation on the face of the globe, even as it struggles to build an empire based on economic power and the threat and use of force, finds itself, from time to time, at the mercy of forces it cannot control, required to negotiate its interests, caught off-guard by the conflicting currents swirling through this incredibly interdependent planetary system.

At the same time, the state becomes the focus of much of the social discontent, anger and frustration that characterize an age in which the old structures are under attack and seem to have lost their vitality, and the new seem too fragile and underdeveloped to carry the weight of meaning being thrust upon them. Secularists and the faithful, ethnic groups and economic interests, the haves and the have-nots focus all their frustrations upon the nation state and struggle to control an institution that is no longer able to meet the demands placed upon it.

Responding to the terrorist attacks in London, Prime Minister Blair may have said more than he intended when he proclaimed that this was not an attack upon one nation, but an attack on all nations.

Indeed, it is the very concept of the nation—a unity forged out of vast and largely irreconciled diversities—that is at stake in the so-called war on terrorism. While the nation state remains a powerful force, one can begin to see out of the corner of the eye, just outside the direct line of sight, the coming of a time when the nation state will be replaced—by a global empire, by a global feudal system, or by some alternative we have yet to envision.

The western world has seen this kind of time before in its history. When Rome dominated the ancient Mediterranean world economically, politically, and militarily, local, indigenous cultures found themselves challenged, uprooted, and dislocated. Religions that had served communities for millennia were forced into confrontation with one another and their abilities to offer meaningful explanations to existence were undermined and dismissed. New religions emerged, constructed out of a mélange of half-remembered, half-understood rituals, myths, and philosophies.

Rome, despite her enormous power found herself fighting unsatis-fying conflicts on the boundaries of empire, conflicts that drained re-sources and undermined the claims of the imperial system. In the end, Rome declared war on Barbarism and entered into a conflict that was ill-defined, and by its very nature endless—a conflict that could only end in the fall of the empire itself. The point of looking at this history is not to suggest that history is repeating itself, but to call our attention to the possibility that patterns may recur.

The conventional wisdom would have it that on September 11, 2001, the world changed irrevocably. It is argued that when airliners filled with people and volatile jet fuel were crashed into the twin towers of the World Trade Center in New York and into the Pentagon in Washington, DC, we entered upon a new era. The world we knew be-fore those events disappeared and the world we have experienced since has been radically different.

However, like all forms of conventional wisdom, this one hides as much as it reveals. In truth, the change to which that terrible moment directed us, did not come in a moment. It has been coming for the last fifty years or more. Unfortunately, our response did not reflect any un-derstanding of the enormity of the challenge that has been gathering force for half a century.

In the immediate aftermath of this attack, the President of the United States reacted in quite a conventional way. He declared war on Terrorism—a term so abstract and general that it is difficult to under-stand how such a war could ever be ended or any victor determined. Fol-lowing from that declaration has come an unfocused struggle, one that is endless, without any way to gauge success, one in which any military ad-venture might be justified. In pursuit of this war on terrorism, the gov-ernment of the United States decided that freedom could only be pro-tected by restricting freedom and that effective international cooperation could be secured only by ignoring the modicum of negotiation and civil-ity that had previously characterized relations among allies. History does not repeat itself, but patterns have a way of recurring.

As the carnage and the destruction began to sink into our consciousness, Americans began asking over and over again, "Why do they hate us so?" Ironically, the message contained in that act of terror was less about Americans than it was about the way the world has changed over the past fifty years, the way cultural and economic changes are seen to have produced spiritual and material impoverishment around the globe. The most important message of that terrible moment was to call us to wake up and see that history has, indeed, become discontinuous and that responding to the challenges of the moment as if nothing much had changed, as if conventional responses like declaring war and exerting force will somehow suffice, is to walk blindly and without direction into a gathering storm.

We live in a time when nothing is decided and everything matters, an era when all the institutions upon which we have relied are shaken and shattered. The church is disappearing even as we watch, to be reincarnated in forms that will seem strange and unfamiliar and bizarre to our eyes. Ancient cultures are being undermined and swept away. The political institutions by which we have structured our lives and to which we have given our loyalties are weakened and tottering. Over fifty years ago, the Welsh-American preacher, A. Powell Davies saw just such a moment bearing down upon us. He left us this advice:

The world we knew is passing,
All things grow strange,
All but the stout heart's courage
All but the undiminished lustre of an ancient dream
Which we shall dream again
As others have dreamed before us,
Children forever of a world forever new.
And what we loved and lost
We lose to find how great a thing is loving
And the power of it to make a dream come true.
For us there is no haven of refuge.

For us there is the wilderness
Wild and trackless,
Where we shall build a road and sing a song.
But after us, there is the promised land,
Strong from our sorrows
Shining from our joys,
Our gift to those who come after us
Along the road we build,
Singing our song.

Without knowing it, without seeing the warning signs, the world has moved into a strange wilderness, wild and trackless. The old structures upon which we have relied to define our place and our meaning are crumbling and disappearing. What will come in their place, none can say.

We are left to sing our songs and to build our roads and to live our lives with courage and integrity and compassion, trusting that the process that brought us to this place, in time, will lead us beyond this wilderness into a new era of hope and promise.

The Very Hardest Thing

Edward Frost, DMin '74

The Unitarian Universalist Congregation of Atlanta

March 2005

In one of the many enduring classic cartoons of James Thurber, his typical poor sad sack of a male is slouched, indolent, defeated in his chair. Two bemused children stand nearby. His wife, fierce and unsympathetic (as Thurber women often are), is saying *"You're* despondent! We're all despondent!"

This is a man whose dreams have not come true, whose bright faith and hope of once-upon-a-time has crumbled beneath realities and harsh truths. And he is despondent. As, so says his cynical spouse, are we all.

Reading David McCullough's marvelous biography of John Adams during my sabbatical, I came across a passage by his beloved daughter, Nabby, a passage that, quite naturally, grew into a sermon. Nabby was twenty-two years old as she wrote this to a friend: "Do you know what the very hardest thing is? The very hardest thing is to hold on to your faith when you discover the truth."

It struck me as being so simple, so obvious a statement and, at the same time, so precociously profound. She had caught the process of maturing faith as precisely as any theologian or preacher could have done. What can we suppose was Nabby's faith that would have been so hard beset by truth?

Young ladies were protected from harsh realities far longer in the early nineteenth century of the Adamses. She would have kept her naiveté, and her faith, intact far longer than our children in this information age bombarded with truths by the hour. The faith of a girl and young woman in the early nineteenth century Massachusetts village of Braintree would have been built by simple Sunday School lessons in the parish church where her grandfather was a deacon.

She would learn first that there is a God and that God is good, never mind the complications of evil yet. She would learn Bible verses by heart. She would learn the basic rules of the Christian life: live by the Beatitudes, the Golden Rule, and the Ten Commandments. Do unto others, as you would have others do unto you. Honor thy father and thy mother.

Only gradually would truths be discovered and come to bear on this simple faith in God's goodness and loving care for his children. Perhaps a beloved pet would be killed by a carriage in the street. Why? Friends, good Christian children, would die of one disease or another. Fire would claim a family just down the road. Bad things would happen to good people. It would not be long before the local pastor's assurances that all this suffering and loss were somehow part of a good God's plan would begin to ring hollow. Moreover, just as the truths of the world begin to weigh in, the truth that our parents are flawed or merely limited also begins to dawn.

As a young woman, Nabby witnessed in disbelief and disillusionment as her beloved father and Thomas Jefferson, a longtime family friend, were pitted against each other in vile politics; each hired the same yellow journalist to smear the other. Politics can put an ugly mask on the sweetest faces.

The very hardest thing is to hold on to one's faith when one begins to discover the truth. In most cases, and in families such as the Adamses, the faith would be maintained by virtue of their willingness to let faith and the truths of daily living live side-by-side, not forcing one upon the other. John Adams said, "Admire and adore the Author of the telescopic universe, love and esteem the work, do all in your power to lessen ill and increase good, but never assume to comprehend." One pocket for faith, another for the truths. It is called "the suspension of disbelief."

Of course Nabby never said it was easy. She said it is the very hardest thing. It has been no easier for us. Whatever our faith is or has been, truths have railed against it, shaking or shattering it, changing it, most certainly, for most of us. "We're all despondent," says Thurber's realist. Depression is, in part, a reaction to loss. I suspect that, to some great extent, at the root of our shared despondency is the accumulation of the losses of chunks of faith we could not save from unavoidable truths. The hardest thing is to maintain one's faith when the truth is discovered.

The poet, ecologist, and farmer, Wendell Berry put it another way: "Be joyous even though you've discovered the facts." What is this, Mr. Berry? "Eat, drink, and be merry, for tomorrow we die?"

What is this faith, so hard to maintain, and what are the truths of our lives in our time? Contemporary liberal faith was perhaps formed in the early part of this century with a generation's almost absolute trust in the future. Wonderful inventions and discoveries abounded. An interval of peace was at hand. They saw the early dawn of social consciousness. It seemed that humankind could only go onward and upward. All boats lifted by the rising tide of good feeling.

And, quoting Shakespeare, "What a piece of work is man; how noble in reason." Humankind, so held the faith, was basically good and would grow naturally more good as modern science made life easier and war unthinkable. All this is summed up by the mantra, "Every day, in every way, I'm getting better and better." A happy thought marketed by a French pharmacist-turned-therapist, perhaps one of the first among the self-help gurus.

The truth? The slaughter of millions in a world war (though it was thought to be the war to end all wars). An influenza epidemic. A great economic depression. And then that which theologians have called the greatest threat to faith in human history: the Second World War and the Holocaust. How could there be a God? And, if there is a God, how could God be good? How could millions of people be slaughtered, how could people slaughter them, if God cares? The problem of evil: How can a good God allow evil, not only to exist, but also to prevail? Right up to the present day, from the holocaust, through September 11, to the continuing mindless killings among Israelis and Palestinians, the liberal faith in the perfectibility of humankind is tested to the breaking point by the daily-demonstrated truths that human beings are capable of just about anything.

The first principle of Unitarian Universalism is "We gather to affirm and promote the inherent worth and dignity of every person." Never mind Hitler, what about Osama Bin Laden? What about the young woman who hit a homeless man and left him impaled for three days in her windshield to die? The truths on every side make it very hard to maintain faith to "affirm" the inherent worth of persons, to proclaim hope for the future.

What is faith? "Faith," says the Christian Scripture, "is the substance of things hoped for. The evidence of things not seen." Faith, then, is not actuality. Faith is not fact or truth. If faith were truth, of course, it wouldn't be faith. To have faith is to have a vision of the future, a vision that may fly in the face of truths, of facts. To have such faith determines how we live in the present.

You remember the story of Job. It is perhaps the oldest story in human history. Job's faith in God's steadfastness was tested by a series of trials in which he lost all his possessions and was left sitting on a dung heap, scratching the sores on his body with a shell. There are actually two endings to that ancient story of Job. The oldest ending, predating Hebrew editing, has Job left with all his suffering and all his losses. Life is what it is. Tough luck, Job. Job's own wife told him to curse God and die. That ending, that truth, was hardly inspiring. The Hebrew editors added a happy ending. For his faithfulness, God restored Job's health, increased his herds a hundred-fold, and blessed his family forever.

It is easy to hold the faith that all is in God's hands, that there is a divine, humanly inscrutable reason for such incomprehensible suffering, all to be revealed and all losses returned in God's good time. Nevertheless, the truths of daily living cannot be ignored by most of us, and faith is hard. The theologian Reinhold Niebuhr wrote, "Nothing worth doing is completed in our lifetime; therefore we are saved by hope. Nothing true or beautiful or good makes complete sense in any immediate context of history; therefore we are saved by faith."

Niebuhr was saying that faith is essential for salvation, salvation meaning being made whole. Faith gives us little proof in our lifetime that how we live will make a difference or that the goodness and beauty we see or that we create will make any sense in the long run. Faith, again, is a vision by which we live without guarantee, which is the very hardest thing.

Let me give you my personal theology of faith and truth. I call it (while waiting for a naming more profound) the "as if" theology of faith. I begin by re-affirming the obvious: that faith, by definition, is not fact. Faith is a declaration. In faith, we declare how life is, what life is, what human nature is, what the future can be. We declare the nature of things in spite of those truths that make faith very hard. We say, for example, in the first principle of Unitarian Universalism, that we affirm the inherent worth and dignity of every person. The term "affirm" indicates that this is not a statement of fact.

We are not confirming that every person is of inherent worth and dignity as if we were going along with an obvious truth. We are affirming it, declaring it. So, to live by faith in the face of those truths we discover that make maintaining faith very hard, is to live as if what we declare about life and the nature of things is true. To live by faith is to live as if. Faith is a choice among alternatives. Looking at the truths—the Holocaust, vicious people, the child abusers—we can choose to live as if human beings are little more than talking beasts doomed to self-annihilation (or Armageddon).

My question is obvious: since we don't know that grimness to be the truth of us, why choose it as an affirmation to live by? Because, make no mistake about it, we will live and behave in our lives by what we declare life and truth to be. In the Christian Scripture attributed to the Apostle James, James says it is simple enough to know what a person's faith is. "By their fruits you shall know them," he said.

If faith is a declaration of the nature of things, why not declare that human life can be improved by our efforts, that what we do makes a difference? Why not live as if that is true? I suppose that is what was intended by Emile Coue—that French pharmacist I mentioned earlier—when he recommended that daily mantra, "Every day, in every way, I'm getting better and better." Why not hold that faith? Why not live as if that were true? What does it serve us to live as if every day, in every way, we are getting worse and worse?

The faith of early childhood is naïve, and perhaps it needs to be. We have other fish to fry in those first years. The disillusionments are also necessary. To mature, we must be able to live with the truths we learn about Santa, fairies, parents, people in general, disease, and death.

As young Nabby wrote to her friend, in the throes of the discoveries we all must make, it is hard to maintain faith when the truth is learned. Yet, if we cannot do that, we must either live in childlike innocence, "the seduction of Peter Pan and of immature religion," or live sadly out of touch with reality entirely. Much of mental illness, after all, stems from the inability to live with the truths.

"We gather to affirm and promote the inherent worth and dignity of every person." That is not a statement of fact. That is an affirmation of faith. And we gather to affirm it and not only to affirm it but also to promote it, to proclaim the faith. It is a declaration we Unitarian Universalists choose to live by. It is an item of our faith.

Yes, there are truths that make it hard. I'm frequently asked, "What about Adolf Hitler; was he of infinite worth and dignity?" I don't know. Probably not. But I will tell you I have stopped struggling with that. I can live with the truths, that is, I can live with apparent exceptions. Why not live as if every person is of inherent worth and dignity? What is the alternative? Surely the "fruits" (the behaviors) of those who live by this faith of the inherent worth of every person result in more good than the fruit of those whose faith is that some people are of infinite worth or that we are all trash destined for hell.

Unitarian Universalism, rightly understood, is not an easy religion and I for one do all in my power to make sure that it neither is nor seems that way. The easy religions are the ones that tell you what to believe. Most of you here were there at some time and it didn't work for you. I tire of hearing that Unitarian Universalists don't have to believe anything. I guess I just don't understand that. Unless you are looking for a date or sales prospects, why would you associate with a religious institution in which you don't have to believe anything? I hope you are not here with the expectation that I am going to affirm that you don't have to believe anything. There are plenty of places to go for companionship in which you don't have to believe anything.

I believe that it is the task of the Unitarian Universalist minister to do the very hardest thing—to proclaim and maintain a faith, while struggling with the truths that, without a faith to live by, would hollow us out and beat us down.

We gather in this circle, around the flame, for warmth against cold, prosaic fact. We gather for the light we can add each other, no single light sufficient. And we gather for the courage we find in community to live by faith, to live by profession and affirmation, to live "as if" in a world of truths we would not cower before but, by the power of faith, transform.

THE DOCTOR IS ALWAYS IN:

LIBERTY AND LIFE IN A
NEW HEALTHCARE PARADIGM

Aaron McEmrys, student

Clinton Unitarian Universalist Fellowship

Clinton, IA

February 2005

Janie is a horse trainer, which she has always seen as more of a calling than a trade. Her job doesn't pay much, less than $10 an hour with no benefits. But for Janie it is a labor of love.

She had been home sick for a couple days and was still feeling weak. Although she suspected she was sicker than usual, she didn't go to the doctor. With no insurance, the only place she could go was the emergency room, and she knew she couldn't pay the bill. So she treated herself as best she could—Echinacea tea, steam bath, and cold medicine.

Later, when Janie stood up from dinner, the room started to spin around her, and a strange roaring sound, like surf pounding on a beach swirled louder and louder as her field of vision shrank to a pinprick before vanishing altogether.

Janie passed out and fell face first against the sharp wooden edge of her bed frame. The full weight of her body crashed down on that frame like an earthquake, with the bridge of her nose as its epicenter. Her face was smashed.

Janie woke up under the bright lights and sterile ferocity of surgery, where a team was trying to reconstruct her face. As soon as she realized where she was, she started struggling, trying to get up off the operating table. As someone rushed to sedate her while others held her still, she kept crying out over and over again—"I have to get out of here. I can't pay! I can't afford to be here, you have to let me go!"

Once she was unconscious again, the team finished putting her face back together. Bills are still trickling in, but so far the tally is roughly $30,000—more than twice what Janie makes in a year.

Janie can't pay. At the time I heard her story, Janie was filing for bankruptcy. She is not alone. Today there are over 40 million people in the United States without health insurance. Forty million is a vast number. Imagine a map of the United States: if all the uninsured people in this country were concentrated in individual states, starting with the least populated states, 24 states would be populated entirely by people without health insurance.

Janie is not alone. Forty million people are one accident, one illness, away from disaster.

Health care reform is not a new topic in Unitarian Universalist circles. We have been working for policy reform for years, and we must continue those efforts. But policy reform alone will not get us where we need to go. We need a paradigm shift.

Our current paradigm is increasingly market-based, where there are no patients, only consumers; and no healers, only suppliers. Health care is a commodity to be purchased by consumers and profited from by shareholders.

Prices are not set by what "health" actually costs, but by the so-called laws of supply and demand. Proponents of this paradigm claim that "free market prices spontaneously and rationally allocate available resources while constraining market participants to live within their means."

"Spontaneously and rationally allocate available resources"… this is not an economic theory, this is a belief system where the market acts like some kind of invisible, infallible, tough-loving god, rewarding the worthy and punishing the unworthy (those who cannot pay).

The assumption here is that consumers purchase health care like any other commodity—because we want it, not because we *need* it. Prices are set based on what the market will bear. Or more accurately, what *we* will bear.

On February 2, 2005, the Chicago Tribune reported that medical bills play a role in over half of all bankruptcies in the United States. These bankruptcies are not just filed by patients who can't pay. They are also filed by members of the patient's families and social networks. Parents adding another mortgage on their home and grandparents liquidating their pensions. These are family values in action.

In 1935, Indian writer Mulk Raj Anand wrote a novel about a boy growing up in India. He was born into the Hindu caste known as the Untouchables. Untouchables are considered polluted. Foul. Even subhuman. They live desperate lives, with no hope, for the future is walled off from them by economic, social and religious strictures. Unsurprisingly, even Untouchables love their children, and it is this love that drives this story, a story about what we, the market, will bear.

A young Untouchable boy named Bakha had been taken by fever, and had been unconscious all night long. Everyone was convinced that Bakha was going to die, but his father Lakha couldn't accept it. Being an untouchable, he was not allowed to go into the Doctor's office, so he stood outside shouting for someone to come out and listen to him.

His voice hoarse from useless shouting, he fell at the feet of everyone who passed the office, begging them to take a message inside "tell the doctor I have a prayer to make to him. My child is suffering from fever. He has been unconscious since last night and he needs medicine!"

"Keep away! Keep away! Do you think I want to have another bath today?!" Not one person would carry Lakha's message.

He stood there on the corner. He had seen shelves of medicine through the side window of the doctor's office and he knew one of those bottles could save his son's life. But he couldn't go in. The medicine might as well have been on another planet.

Lakha was sure his son was dying, and was torn between waiting outside the office and wanting to see his son's face one more time before he died. Lakha ran home and cradled his son's head in his lap. The little boy opened his eyes and looked at his father, but was too delirious to recognize him.

Lakha snapped. He ran back to the doctor's office and did not stop at the door. He threw himself at the feet of the doctor and said, "still, there is a little life left in my child's body. If you save him I will be your slave all my life—please—the meaning of my life is my child!"

There was havoc in the doctor's office. All the patients bolted to escape the taint of the untouchable. Hundreds of rupees worth of medicine were polluted by Lakha's mere presence. The doctor aimed a furious kick, but Lakha took the doctor's boot and placed it on his head, closed his eyes, and waited.

After a long pause, the doctor relented and went to treat the boy. The treatment was successful and the boy lived. Right now, in our country, there are 40 million people who, like Lakha, have to wait outside the doctors' office hoping for a miracle.

Healthcare is not a commodity. Prices cannot be set on what the market will bear because it will bear—*we* will bear—everything. We are not isolated individuals. We are mothers and brothers and friends and lovers and children—and we are bound together by love. And love is more valuable to us than life itself. There is no price too high to save the life of someone we love. The market will bear everything, until nothing is left.

It's time for a new paradigm, one based on the inherent worth and dignity of all. A new paradigm where health is not a commodity but a human right.

Paradigm shifts don't just happen, but are driven by agents of change. We Unitarian Universalists must be among these agents of change, midwives at the birth of a new health paradigm.

For too long, policy decisions have revolved around how much money is "available." How much it costs is the wrong question—how much did it cost to abolish slavery? Human rights transcend economics. The effects of this paradigm shift will be earthshaking.

There is a migrant health clinic I know that is saving lives with stories. Since the 1970s this clinic has been the only clinic for miles around that will treat uninsured migrant and immigrant workers. The recent recession in this country hit the clinic's service area especially hard, but despite the ever-increasing patient load, the government kept cutting their funding. Everybody just kept taking on more work, as if the gaping holes in the budget could be filled with pure will.

As the country sank deeper into recession, the clinic was notified that it was slated to lose almost its entire operating budget. It would mean the end of health care for hundreds of patients, most of whom were women and children.

But then a group of people who worked for the clinic started to organize. They started interviewing patients and staff about what the clinic meant to them and to their community, and collected stories of miracles and tragedies. And, as all these stories started coming together, people began to realize that they were all part of the same big story.

Many of the patients and staff are religious, so it seemed natural to begin sharing this story in their churches. The story started to take on life for lots of people, not just the people who were experiencing it directly. It started to belong to the whole community. Before long they were setting up meetings with legislators to tell the story of the clinic. And it wasn't a priest talking with a legislator about what his parishioners were going through. The priest might be there for support, but the stories came directly from the people, many of whom were claiming— liberating—their voices for the first time: women from Mexico, Honduras, Guatemala, El Salvador and many other places.

The state backed away from its cuts, and the clinic survived. But that was just the beginning. People came together in ways they never had before; they started feeling new power and possibility. They changed public policy, but they also gave birth to a new paradigm, right in their little corner of rural America. The story is different there now.

A paradigm shift like this isn't going to happen in Washington, DC. The stories of the lobbyists and politicians drift ever further from our own. If there is to be a shift, we have to make it. People will stand up, they will put their shoulders to the wheel of change, but not because of an article they read. People will stand up when there is a story that includes them, a story that gives them a new world to strive for.

In these days of war, injustice and violence abroad, it is all too easy to overlook the everyday injustice and violence in our own communities, but look at it we must. The paradigmatic struggle for a new healthcare story is a struggle for the right to live—that most fundamental of liberties. There are 40 million lives at stake, and the casualties mount every day. And, as in most struggles, those casualties fall most heavily where they always have—among women and children, whose voices have been silenced for too long.

We need to start gathering stories—our own stories and the stories of others because after all, that's what paradigms are made of. No story is too small to make a difference, and no voice is too soft to be heard. We need to be guided by stories of family doctors watching over the beds of sick children just as much as we need stories from the people who stand outside. We need a paradigm defined by what we are reaching for even more than by what we are struggling against.

We can start with sharing our stories right here. Start within this congregation, but don't stay within it. Reach out. Envision a world where no one is untouchable, and the Doctor is always in.

OUT FROM WALDEN

Patrick T. O'Neill, DMin '79

The Service of the Living Tradition

2005 General Assembly of the Unitarian Universalist Association

Ft. Worth, Texas

June 2005

Dedication

Listed among the roll of ministers remembered this evening in the year of their death is the name of my first Unitarian Universalist minister, the Rev. David Osborn, whose wife and partner for his many years of ministry, Janet, also died this year. Some thirty-three years ago, it was at their dinner table in Oradell, New Jersey, that I first shared my secret longing to become a minister. I dedicate this sermon in love and everlasting gratitude to David and Janet's memory.

When I found myself enrolled in theological school in Chicago a year after that fateful, confessional dinner at the Osborns' home, our great Unitarian Universalist professor James Luther Adams reminded us in his church history class that the word "tradition" in church history can be translated with two very different meanings in Latin. The first root word of tradition is "traditum," a heavy-sounding word, which means "the unchanging inherited weight and authority of history."

But a second, much lighter translation of tradition is the Latin word, "traditio," meaning "a sense of the living customs of a community; the ongoing creative dance of ever-evolving meaning and practice."

As illustration of the difference between *traditum* and *traditio*, James Luther Adams offered us the larger-than-life example of Tevya, the devout dairyman of Anatevka, in *Fiddler on the Roof.* When first we meet Tevya, he explains to us that tradition—the heavy obligation of *traditum*—determines virtually every aspect of his family's life and his life as a man, as a husband, and absolutely as a Papa.

But as the story unfolds, we watch how this good man's tradition-bound heart is repeatedly and ultimately challenged and overruled by his love for his three daughters, and we listen in on his anxious conversations with God as his independent-minded daughters, one by one, teach him the primacy of love over custom. They, teach him to choose L'Chaim, Life, the dance of *traditio*, as the highest ultimate reckoning with his heritage. He explains to God his daughter Tzeitel's decision to marry for love rather than by arrangement: "They gave each other a pledge—unthinkable. But look at my daughter's face—how she loves him ... and look at my daughter's eyes—so hopeful." Tradition!

Here in this annual Service of the Living Tradition, wherein our collective community of memory and of hope is evoked and named in the line of our ministry saluting both the generation who precede us in service and now recognizing those ready to take up the mantle of ministry, in this revered ritual we reference both meanings of tradition: both the pride and weighty rich inheritance of five centuries tracing back to the 16th century in Transylvania and beyond; and at the same time, we take up our own generation's obligation to define and refine constantly for ourselves the norms and practice of our living covenant in the free church.

For, like Tevya, as we hold dear the precious legacy handed down to us, so we recognize that we exist as churches, as free-faith communities, and as those ordained to work in the name of this legacy, we recognize that we exist to serve and to make better the tenor of our times, to give meaning to our days. These particular times, I mean; and these particular days. The times we are given to live and to shape. The days that have our names on them.

As a living community we take up the dance of *traditio*. At its best, it can be a communal choreography capable of almost balletic grace and harmony; even if, at other times, it more resembles a crazy tarantella, with all of us bumping into each other and stomping on each others' toes, all in the clumsy, sometimes comical improvisation of community that is the living church.

What lends the free church both constant power and constant challenge, of course, is it's unique placement as that city on the hill that is always both part of society and prophet to that society. It has been the nature of our church and its ministry from time immemorial always to wrestle with a kind of schizoid tendency to shift back and forth between full-blown retreat from the world on the one hand, offering itself as sanctuary and refuge from the world—and full-blown engagement and confrontation with the world on the other hand. The church as comforter of our afflictions and haven in our struggles, on the one hand; the church as afflicter of our comfort and poker of our conscience, on the other. The church as righteous prophet, demanding our efforts to mend what is broken in the world; to heal what is wounded in our communities; to hold gently the sorrows and to address lovingly the pain of those perennially left out on the margins of society; the hopeless and the helpless; the war-torn and the hungry and the infected of the world.

Perhaps no one figure in our history more personally incarnates the push and pull of our Unitarian Universalist dance between retreat and engagement with the world than our beloved idealist, Henry David Thoreau, who in his intentional withdrawal from society into the woods of Walden Pond for two years appeals to one very deep historic strain of Unitarian Universalist sensibility; while his great essay on "Civil Disobedience" and his willingness to be jailed as an anti-war and Abolitionist tax protester makes him a hero in another chamber of the Unitarian Universalist heart.

On this occasion, this evening when we ponder the sum and substance of our Living Tradition, it is to Thoreau's life and writings which we might profitably turn for one source of inspiration and illumination. In his relatively short life—Thoreau died at age 45 remember—he penned a personal journal of some two million words explaining both the idealistic principles that he went into the woods to discover and to ponder, but also, lest we forget, the demands of a highly developed moral conscience that eventually called him out of the woods to actively engage in abolitionist confrontation with his society.

When he moved into his rough-hewn cabin on Walden Pond on the outskirts of Concord on the Fourth of July, 1845, Thoreau wrote his immortal apologia for retreating into the sanctuary of Natural surroundings far from the madding crowd:

> *"I went to the woods because I wished to live deliberately, to front only the essential facts of life, and see if I could not learn what it had to teach, and not, when I came to die, discover that I had not lived."*

When Thoreau came out from Walden two years later in 1847, he wrote, "I left the woods for as good a reason as I went there. Perhaps it seemed to me that I had several more lives to live, and could not spend any more time for that one."

It was not until seven years after he left the woods that Thoreau finally published Walden to great acclaim. But in the years in between his leaving the woods and publishing his famous account of why he went there, it was his essay on "Civil Disobedience" which gained his reputation. After the Fugitive Slave Act was passed in 1851, it was the work of Abolitionism, and involvement in Underground Railroad activity, and lecturing on "Slavery in Massachusetts" that occupied much of Henry's time and thought. When the rabid Abolitionist John Brown visited Concord in 1857, Thoreau was among the Transcendentalist circle that first welcomed him and helped promote Brown's "radical chic" notoriety in the face of the federal government's continued cooption by the system, both North and South, that maintained Slavery as an institution.

While he never lost his vocation as a Naturalist and botanist, neither did Thoreau ever lose his prophetic idealism for the great justice issues of his day. His spirituality, nurtured in periods of pensive solitude and in his daily ramblings in the countryside, and which he recorded in a voluminous daily journal over the years, was eventually formative of Henry's fierce moral conscience, a conscience always unafraid to speak truth to power; to take a stand for principle; to name the evils that afflicted his day. What a powerful icon he remains, what a shining example for what we in the free church might aspire to in our own time!

Alas, it has been suggested by some that, of late, over the last twenty or thirty years now, liberal religion itself has been in something of a Waldenesque retreat from effective activist engagement in the crucial moral struggles of our time. As more and more of our churches moved out from the environs of our great urban centers and relocated themselves quite literally into the exurban woods and fields of suburbia (the better to serve the majority of a membership that consequently remains overwhelmingly white, middle-to-upper class, and educationally elite), it has been suggested by some that we in the liberal church tradition have been too long enamored with the ideal of Thoreauvian retreat from the mix and mess of the world, and that we have been too little mindful of Thoreau's later example of conscientiously speaking up, speaking out, acting up, and acting out in behalf of the causes of righteousness in our culture.

It is said by some critics that liberal religion has seemed to lose much of its voice, if not its way altogether, if not its righteous indignation in the face of social and moral causes that once would have lit up our pulpits in moral outrage. The charge has been leveled that liberal religion has gone all but mute, in far too many places, in behalf of causes that once (at least we like to think) would have pulled our people out of the pews, put their feet in motion, and put their hands to work reclaiming the proper contours of that ancient city on the hill, the one we once imagined: that dreamt-of society where racism, economic injustice, and war-mongering are named for the blights that they are upon the human soul.

Dare we hope to find again, in this newest generation of ministers, preachers who burn with unapologetic indignation in behalf of equal opportunity, equal education, equal health care, decent housing for everyone, the equal right of every person to marry whomever they love, and the right of every woman to be the sole decider of what happens to her body? Dare we look to you newest ministers of our Living Tradition for preaching and teaching that will pour concrete foundations under the moral arguments for a just society, for a world at peace?

For these are moral human issues before ever they are social policies, no matter what party is in power, no matter who happens to be sitting in the White House, or sitting in Congress, or sitting on the Supreme Court. Our ministry has no moral right not to speak to these issues, no matter whom we might offend or make uncomfortable in our pews! Whether such preaching grows our membership or not, whether it is effective institutional strategy for our Association or not, these are the issues that will always determine the health and integrity of liberal religion, or what's a pulpit for?

What's a pulpit for?

Tonight as we speak, for example, from our privileged place in the midst of an almost obscenely wealthy nation, it is simply shameful, a moral travesty, that upwards of thirty million children under the age of fifteen in America have no medical insurance.

We should rush home from this General Assembly and carve the words, "Leave No Child Behind" into every pulpit in the Unitarian Universalist Association, until we take that sacred phrase back from those who now use it as a sarcastic euphemism and give it back to Marion Wright Edelman who knows how to live it and mean it! If we're looking to reclaim our pulpit fire, here's one place to start!

To you young colleagues who are the focus for this service, who tonight are officially invested at the beginning of your ministries, oh, how we welcome you! And how we need you to take up your work with passion and the determination to make your mark! For, Brothers and Sisters, I come to announce to you some rather alarming news tonight: Walden is burning! The woods, our beloved woods, are on fire! Our Eden, our idyllic retreat, our sylvan sanctuary from the mundane cares of the world, Eden is ablaze tonight!

Every one of you who dons the stole of ministerial office tonight is hereby called to action. All Idyllic weekend passes are hereby cancelled, and you are to report immediately to these pulpits, or to the community agencies that you serve, to your chaplaincies, to the classrooms where you teach, to the communities where your voice is respected, where your leadership is counted upon. Walden, our beloved liberal religious haven from the world, Walden is on fire! And it is time for more Unitarian Universalists to catch fire too.

I cannot urge you enough, if you take up the ministry at this point in our history, young colleagues, be aware: do not take on this mantle merely to save your own soul. Rather, we need you to become ministers, as the poet urges, to spend your souls, spend them lavishly and wantonly in service to the world. I entreat you, do not use your trusted office to take refuge while the world around you is going to hell. Do not employ your preaching talents to give comfort to the already too comfortable.

We do not need in our pulpits at this point in our history any more retreatants. Or dilettante scholars. Or idle poets. I implore you, do not seek here amid these thousand-plus congregations for ministries of quietude, or for more churches in the woods, where you can take shelter in theological reverie while the social policies of our country are increasingly determined to protect the already privileged and to ignore the already deprived. The woods are lovely, dark, and deep, but you have promises to keep! The liberal ministry of our time needs ministers with fire in the belly, fire in the eye, and fire in the heart.

Ignite, young colleagues, I beseech you! Catch fire! Or better you should never put on the stole, please.

Martin Luther King, Jr. said that he kept a dog-eared copy of Thoreau's *Civil Disobedience* in his car, and he memorized long passages from it to pass his time in jail. "I read Thoreau's words," he said, "to center my spirit and to re-find my purpose, and then my courage is restored and my vision is again made clear." Would that we learn to do the same with but a portion of his courage and his effectiveness!

Our prayer for you this night, you duly fellowshipped colleagues taking up your ancient calling (a calling that will cost you everything you have, a profession that will humble you, that will break your hearts even as it gives meaning and purpose to your lives) and as you assume your earned place in the line of Channing and Murray and Ballou and Brown, the line of Parker and Priestley, the line of Joseph Tuckerman, the line of the Iowa Sisterhood, the line of Safford and Gordon and Blackwell, of Helvie and Padgham, the line later of Lewis McGee, of Fahs and Holmes and Skinner and Davies, the line of Jim Adams, the line of David Osborn and a thousand other ministers before you, most of them unfamous and uncelebrated, but all the saints whose good lives once gave sheen and luster to this heritage and whose spirits fill this hall tonight to applaud with us as you walk across this stage, our prayer: What they dreamed be *yours* to do!

May your fire bring us out, dear colleagues, lead us out from the safe Waldens where liberal religion has been too long in hiding, too long asleep, too long comfortable and complacent! Lead us out! Lead us!

Remember, and never let anyone forget, that you are not ordained to become just some under-glorified business manager of a local religious franchise measuring your ministry's worth in numbers or in bottom lines. And your church's role and function is never merely to serve as just another perennially underfunded non-profit agency in town. The church's reason for being is to make real the Beloved Community on earth, nothing less. And your office in all its varied forms, exists to embody the work of that ideal, nothing less.

Thirty years on, James Luther Adams's words still echo true. The Covenant, the Covenant, the Covenant, he insisted, is the great glowing coal at the heart of our free church tradition. Preach the covenant, then, *traditum* and *traditio*, binding us one with another and with our God.

Preach the covenant then, first and last, binding us one with the world beyond our walls, in all its woundedness and imperfection.

Preach the covenant, binding us to Channing's faith and to Murray's dream, to Theodore's fire, and to Olympia's courage; binding us, binding us always, to Jim Reeb's immortal heart.

Preach to us the covenant bravely and fearlessly, my new colleagues, and in your preaching know that you will be forever blessed in the sight of that which causes the sparrow to fly and the lilies of the field to bloom. Preach the covenant, binding us with the sacred center of life: whose love is finally our only doctrine, whose quest for truth remains our precious sacrament, and whose service is evermore our fervent and lasting prayer. Still.

Amen and Amen

How To Name Your Farm

Valerie Mapstone Ackerman, MDiv '98

The big red dog is gone. He sat in the sun near me all day that final Monday, basking in the warmth, checking in with an occasional lick to my ear and then settling back into the turf. Young-red-dog Lydia scampered in the next field challenging the cattle to a dance in which they had no interest.

If I had known it would be our last day together, I would have dropped the pecan gathering to spend the afternoon stroking Big Guy's ears and scratching his chest just the way he liked.

As the sun set and the chill wind rattled the branches, I decided to pack up and head inside. Along the way I filled the dog bowls with cheap food and checked the water. If I had known this would be his last meal, I would have taken a moment to break an egg on top of Big Guy's bowl. Makes a dog's fur shine, I hear.

But I didn't know. How could I know that his front porch straw-padded house would be empty the next morning? How could I know that I would spend Tuesday walking the fields then driving up and down the back-country roads searching for his familiar tail and baritone bark. "Maybe," I thought, "He's gone off to his previous home just down the road." No sign of him there. Perhaps he was insulted and indignant after being teased with several nights spent indoors when the temperature plunged only to be locked out onto the front porch for the warming trend.

My husband assured me that he was fine. "He can take care of himself. He was a stray when he moved in. He probably went off with a pack of dogs to hunt," Bill insisted.

It was true. There were packs of dogs roaming the hills. I'd seen them skirt the edges of the fields. Once a tangle of them tumbled into the front yard—beautiful white shaggy types and sleek yellow dogs with curled tails and black and tan mongrels. Big Guy and Lydia welcomed them, sharing favorite chew toys (empty soda bottles mostly).

One white dog seemed especially tame. Tail wagging, almost grinning, he approached me near the farm gate. Out of nowhere Big Guy barreled in growling, shoulder fur standing up. He nipped lightly at the white dog's front paws. "It's okay, Big Guy. He's a sweet little fellow," I said, patting Big Guy's head. But that was it. Big Guy had established the parameters for further visits: play with my comrade, play with the toys, but no touching my human.

A couple of times that week I spotted wild dogs in packs. My heart skipped a beat as I recognized Big Guy trailing with one pack, but as I slowed my chili-pepper red Jeep and looked again, I found that the tail wasn't right. Too curly.

And what would I do exactly if it *was* Big Guy? I already knew he wouldn't get into the Jeep. How many times I had tried to lure him in, shove him in, cajole, sweet-talk, or entice him with treats? He was too big and too independent to be forced. Usually, I could reason with him, but never about the Jeep. Didn't I know moving vehicles were the enemy? One shouts at them, occasionally chases them, definitely sprinkles the tires, but *never* does one ride inside.

Many times I sat Big Guy down to have a discussion about his health and well being. "See, if we put this purple flea collar on, you'll scratch less." Nothing doing. No sooner did I get it on than he ran away across the fields and stayed away the whole afternoon. He came back at dusk sans flea collar. Okay, so no flea collar.

Next I tried to talk him into spray-on treatment. He won that struggle by rubbing it all off on the grass in a frenzied wriggle. How about the veterinarian-recommended skin penetrating treatment for fleas and ticks? I won that battle the old-fashioned way—I made my husband do it.

When we brought Lydia home last Memorial Day, Big Guy established his dominance with one big growl. Not that there was any question about top-dog status. We picked Lydia as an act of kindness; drove all the way to Poteau then up into a rutted holler road to find the breeder. Sleek champion-bred, five-month-old, redbone coonhounds strutted and romped all over the yard. The lone little girl dog trembled slightly, holding back. I came there with no pre-conceived idea of which dog to pick. I didn't even know if I wanted a male or female. But this little dog needed us. Her big brothers dominated her, pushed her around, cut her off from meeting the new humans. Having grown up the lone girl with five brothers, I immediately felt an affinity. Besides, no way was this frightened puppy ever going to be a good hunting dog.

Clearly she needed to be our pampered pet. The ride home confirmed her delicate nature. She drooled and peed and even threw up for good measure. By the time we got home she had a name that came from my desire for an elegant historic name combined with Bill's love of puns. "Lydia" for Ralph Waldo Emerson's wife and "Lid-ea" for the fact that Bill first spotted her carrying a lid from an ice cream bucket.

Without a doubt Big Guy was top dog. Not just the boss—he was Lydia's teacher, too, and her disciplinarian. When I'd scold Lydia for pulling clothes off the laundry line, or chewing the porch furniture, Big Guy would rush in, put her down by the neck and bark ferociously. As long as Big Guy was around to reinforce the message, Lydia quickly learned the family rules.

Sometimes we would translate Big Guy's barks. "Hey you silly mutt, we've got a good thing going here, don't blow it!" or "How many times does she need to tell you this?!" or "Listen, bitch. Do not *eat* the furniture!"

Big Guy came with the farm. He had moved in when the previous owners' Weimaraner bitch had gone into heat. They told us that the folks down the way had begun feeding him about five years ago and then last fall he made his opportunistic relocation. Mr. Gray said he'd surely try to shoo him off if we liked, but by then I was already in love. And it was mutual. Big Guy and I bonded from the first moment our eyes met—maybe not quite the first moment. He always barked fiercely at any vehicle entering the property and he did intimidate me the first time our realtor brought us by to look at the land and house. Later, in the spring after the sale was set up and I came by to visit before the final exchange, Big Guy and I had a moment of mutual understanding in which I gave him permission to stay and he gave me permission to move in.

As bossy and scary as Big Guy might seem, he was also the most gentle and intelligent dog I have ever met. When our equally bossy and scary super-intelligent six-year-old granddaughter came to visit for the whole summer, Big Guy sensed he had met his match. He both protected Keegan and gave her a wide berth. He even allowed Keegan to give him a special name: Clifford, The Big Red Dog. She called him Clifford, or Red, or Big Guy. It didn't matter. He would come when called and sit on command and let Keegan, whom he outweighed by at least 20 pounds, hug his neck and scratch his belly. Though she probably earned it a hundred times, never once did Big Guy growl or raise his hackles at her.

And now he's gone. Just gone—as though he never existed.

Since he wouldn't wear one I can't take his smelly collar and tuck it away in a box like some sentimental fool. I can't bury his broken body with prayers and readings, singing, and a special marker. He didn't die of illness or old age. He didn't just run away, I know it. Somewhere in these hills or valleys he intruded upon the wrong people, spooked the wrong livestock. How could they know his bark was (mostly) a big attitude earned the hard way? How could they know his dog-soul held secrets of love and affection?

I have my memories and a few snapshots. Lydia is still here, as sweet and graceful as ever and adjusting well to Molly the Manic Black Lab we adopted from a shelter on New Year's Eve. Lydia showed us that she needed a companion by ripping off the front screen door then break-ing into the house the night after Big Guy disappeared.

Bill can't bring himself to admit Red (as he called Big Guy) is really gone.

Our FedEx lady and I cried together the last time she came by, ready to hand out dog treats for Christmas.

For months we've been trying to figure out what to call our farm. A while ago Bill suggested "Red Dog Farm." I thought it was just silly. Now though, that name feels fitting, like the memorial I never got to have.

Red Dog Farm it is—for Big Guy.

Entertaining Strangers

Douglas Taylor, MDiv '99

Unitarian Universalist Congregation

Binhgamton, NY

April 2005

This week, I spent Wednesday, Thursday and Friday up in Niagara Falls. I was attending the Annual Spring retreat for the ministers and religious educators from all over the Saint Lawrence District. It was good to be in the company of colleagues; I always find that refreshing. The topic for the workshop portion of the retreat was continuing education along the lines of diversity training and anti-oppression work. Now, workshops on this sort of thing can be transformative and life-changing—the first or second time you do it. Unfortunately, it can also be tedious and annoying after you've been at what seems to be the same stuff a dozen times or more. It was so nice to find a new approach offered; a new path into understanding the complexity of engaging with people and communities of people who have a fundamentally different identity from my own.

Really, what multiculturalism and anti-oppression efforts are based on is the ability for me to meet and engage with people who are in some way different from me. It is about recognizing and honoring each other's differences. We should be great at this, don't you think? We Unitarian

Universalists are all about honoring individual differences. Unfortunately the work of really honoring and welcoming those who are different is not easy to 'just do.' It takes an almost radical component that seems to be in short supply these days.

I want to share with you the opening exercise we did during the workshop. The leader called it the "Culture Toss" game. She handed out papers that had twelve empty blocks, each labeled with a different identity category. For example, 'gender' was one of the identity categories: that I am male is a defining feature of my identity. Race/ethnicity, culture, language, sexual orientation, denominational affiliation, highest values, and roles were all on this list, too.

What roles do you fill that give definition to your identity? I fill the roles of father and husband, minister, and friend. These roles help define who I am, help determine my identity. On this paper, we were filling in the specifics of our different identity characteristics. We had twelve categories, and we were given about ten minutes to fill it all out. Some of that was easy. Gender: male; sexual orientation: straight; race/ethnicity: Irish and mixed northern European; language: American English.

Some of it was harder. For my culture I wrote down: New York/ New England almost-middle-class liberal. For vocation I put down both parenthood and ministry. There was a category for possessions. What possessions give some definition to my identity? I finally wrote in: my guitar, my books, and my socks.

So, with our charts filled out, we were then asked to cross out four of the twelve. Find four identity categories you could live without, or rather, that you would be least troubled to lose. Well, it took some of us a while to wrap our brains around that. I can imagine what it might be like if suddenly it became illegal to be Unitarian Universalist or to speak English. But take something like 'gender,' how could I lose being male? Would that mean there would be no more men? The leader helped clarify by saying, "Maybe it means that it is no longer acceptable to be male or to be white."

I started crossing out my four categories. She didn't give us enough time. After ditching my possessions and my defining habits (no more singing loud in public or drinking coffee), I decided I could stand to learn a new language anyway. Well, I had three and time was up, so I quickly scanned my paper and decided (I'm a little ashamed to say) to cross out Unitarian Universalism.

Now, let me explain: I figured Unitarian Universalism is already an unacceptable religion in many people's eyes, and if it became illegal to be Unitarian Universalist, I figured we could continue to meet in private or we could slowly take over a nice Methodist church.

It turns out that was the easy part. Imagining four identity categories of my own choosing removed from my life was the easy part. Now we turn our papers over to the person we've been paired up with and they get to remove four more identity categories. The only consolation is that while my colleague is taking away my culture and my sexual orientation I get to do the same to him (except after I'm done, he is not allowed to be a "him" anymore).

Now I was asked to sit back and imagine my life without these foundational identity markers. It's illegal to speak English; Unitarian Universalism has gone underground; the New England liberal middle-class is dead; people avoid me if I start to sing loud in public; and they whisper if I'm seen drinking coffee. My books are gone and stores just don't sell crazy socks anymore. I can still be a white male, but I have to be in the closet about my heterosexuality. The one loss that hit me the hardest was not being allowed to have my vocations: ministry and parenthood.

I began to be able to imagine what it might have been like to be a slave. My language and my culture, gone; my religion, crushed; my family, broken up and sold off to different places; no possessions; and I certainly cannot sing loud in public! And all of that has not even touched on ethnicity and skin color. Anyone who thinks racism is all about skin color just doesn't get it.

The point of this exercise was to begin to understand what the experience of being oppressed might be like. The point was to stretch my understanding and open my mind up to what it might be like to be someone of an oppressed culture. The point was opening people to differences. The basic critical component to honoring and welcoming those who are in some fundamental way different from you is in your ability to understand their experiences. It is to be able to put yourself inside their shoes and walk around in them for a while.

The story of Passover for the Jewish people is the story of freedom and liberation. Passover is celebrated every year and during the Seder meal the story is told again. And the piece of it that touches the experiences I had this week with the Anti-oppression work is the way the story of Passover serves as a reminder of Jewish identity, a reminder of the ways in which that identity can be lost, and the powerful call to therefore be hospitable. "Do not ill-treat the stranger in your midst," God says. "Remember, you once were strangers in Egypt." Recently, Michelle Medwin, the Rabbi at Temple Concord, was the religion guest columnist in the *Press & Sun Bulletin*. She wrote about the meaning of Passover. "We are told to see this story as if we, ourselves, were slaves," she wrote. "This teaches us to reach out to the stranger, rather than be fearful of him. It also reminds us that we must reach out to those who are oppressed."

There is one word that is particularly vital to understanding people who are in some way different; one word that allows for the hospitality toward strangers to be real and authentic. It is more that just remembering. The word is imagination. As Einstein said "Imagination is more important than intelligence." Imagination is the critical piece of recognizing and honoring differences.

There is no way to fully understand another person's experiences. You know your own experiences. Someone may be able to tell you about his or her experiences but we can't fully understand them the way we like to think we can. In a very real way we are each isolated within our own experiences. I can only know what is going on from my perspective. You can tell me what you see and experience, but I have to filter what you tell me through the only connection I have with the world, and that is my own experiences.

And that would be a dire scenario if that really were the end of the story; but all is not lost. There is hope through imagination. Imagination builds a bridge between what I know of my experiences and what you share with me of yours. There has been some very scholarly philosophy grown up around ideas like this. I recall one author whom I was assigned to read in seminary, David Tracy. Tracy wrote about Analogical Imagination as the critical component to understanding one another, the base work of communication with any depth. This is why so much of religious language is built upon metaphors. I have an experience and then use analogy to help you imagine what my experience was like.

Imagination is the critical piece for all this. Now, here is what I don't mean by *imagination*. I don't use the word in the sense of *imaginary*. I don't use the word to mean making things up or making conclusions based on little or no facts, as in "You're letting your imagination run away;" or "you have an over-active imagination." Instead I mean imagination as the ability to deal creatively with reality. It is the ability to imagine new possibilities based on, though beyond, what we already know.

We are each different. Modern American Unitarian Universalism is certainly structured around the recognition of that truth. Each one of us is a unique individual. We affirm and promote the inherent worth and dignity of each individual. We vest a great amount of authority in the individual religious conscience, proclaiming that you and you alone can discern, through your own free and responsible searching, what is ultimately true and meaningful. However, as Jonathan Sacks wrote in *The Dignity of Difference*, "the challenge of the religious imagination is to see God's image in one who is not in our image." The challenge is for us to have imagination enough to get outside ourselves enough to see another person's perspective.

The analogy of eyesight applies well. Depth perception is gained by having two eyes focused on the same object. If you close one eye, it is very difficult to judge depth and distance. A depth of understanding is gained by having more than one perspective focused on the same issue. Listening to the perspectives of others will lead you to a deeper understanding of yourself and your world.

Imagination is the ability to envision new possibilities based on, though beyond, what we already know. This is what is happening in the Seder meal when people retell the Passover story to remind themselves of what they already know and to imagine new possibilities. Listening to another person's perspective, entertaining another person's ideas, helps you appreciate your own understanding at a deeper level. By imagining it from another person's point of view, you become open to new ways of seeing and understanding.

The presenter of the anti-oppression workshop shared a story. She talked about a time during her chaplaincy as a student minister in a hospital. She and the other student chaplains were debriefing experiences of their work. The one person of color in the group began talking about how difficult it sometimes was to be a black chaplain in an otherwise surprisingly segregated hospital. Other student chaplains, trying to be helpful, expressed their understanding of his situation. "I understand what you're going through. It is terrible." The woman—who, at that point, had no training yet of the sort she was offering us—continued the story by telling us that she had looked at the man and said, "I have no idea what it must be like for you. I have never had black skin." The man responded to her as if she were his best friend.

I don't know what it is like to have a parent die. I don't know what it is like to get divorced. I don't know what it must feel like to walk into this church for the first time looking for a religious home. I don't know what it is like to be threatened simply for being openly gay. I don't know what it is like to be Latina. I don't know what it is like to be put in prison. I don't know. I have never experienced any of those things. I can, however, gain enough of an understanding of each of those, because I have experienced many other painful things and I know how to listen and I have a good imagination.

This is what it takes to dismantle oppression, but that is not all that this can do. Using your imagination is what it takes to overcome otherwise insurmountable differences between people, but that is not all it can do. Your imagination is critical to engage in religious dialogue of any consequence with other people of good will, but that is not all it is for. I believe the imagination must be at the root of any relationship in your life. Imagination is the ability to deal creatively with reality. Reality always has troubles, and the quickest and easiest way to deal with trouble is usually unimaginative and unhelpful.

Stretch yourself, imagine a new possibility. Listen to other people, entertain strangers in your midst, and stay open to the hope of new being bursting into your life in ways you've never imagined.

In a world without end, may it be so.

Living in Gratitude

Stephen Atkinson

Ministerial Intern

First Unitarian Church of Dallas

Timberland Unitarian Universalist Fellowship

Lufkin, TX

November 2005

Gratitude. It's almost a cliché, isn't it? A lot of us think, "I'm grateful for stuff. Sure I am." Well, gratitude is a simple idea, but it's not easy.

Gratitude requires constant spiritual practice.

The film *Pollyanna* was one of Hayley Mills' greatest roles. Pollyanna is an orphan, but she never feels sorry for herself; her parents had been poor missionaries in the West Indies, but they'd taught her to be grateful for even the smallest pleasures. Once orphaned, she comes to live with an aunt who is rich, but nevertheless stubborn and bitter. Pollyanna chooses to love her anyway and to be grateful for her generosity. As Pollyanna gets to know people in the town, many of them unhappy, she always carries her parents' message: there is always something to be grateful for.

An old hypochondriac, Mrs. Snow, played by Agnes Moorehead,

stays in bed constantly thinking of death. Pollyanna shows Mrs. Snow how to make rainbows with prisms hung in the window; she also brings her quilting squares so she can contribute to the town bazaar to raise funds for a new orphanage. When Mrs. Snow claims to be too weak to sew, Pollyanna, in a rare fit of temper, confronts her fakery and tells her she should be grateful just to be alive, instead of planning her funeral all the time. After Pollyanna storms out, Mrs. Snow picks up the squares and asks for her sewing kit. Later, she actually goes to the bazaar to dish out ice cream. That's the kind of effect Pollyanna had, charming and innocently shaming people into feeling better.

Bit by bit, her optimism in the face of every problem changes the whole town. When her aunt forbids Pollyanna to attend the bazaar, she sneaks out her third-story window and down a tree; she has an essential part to play in the town pageant as the middle piece of the flag and a solo in "America the Beautiful!" Afterwards, trying to climb back in her window, Pollyanna falls, literally off the roof and figuratively into her own slough of despond; her legs are paralyzed. Now, those whose lives she has changed come to give her back her own medicine: they help her to be glad again, first by helping her be glad for their good news, and then to help her feel some hope of recovering. Even her sour aunt is converted as Pollyanna is carried off for surgery in Baltimore. I tell you there wasn't a dry eye in my house. I saw it again recently, and I, a wised-up, post-midlife-crisis, seen-and-heard-it-all guy, loved it all over again.

But, I'm in seminary now. I'm supposed to figure out why things have meaning for me. I asked myself what was it about this movie that made such an impression on me as a child. Could I have had a sense of how important gratitude would become in my life?

I learned about gratitude from real people who had 'fallen off the roof:' the broken, joyous souls at twelve-step meetings. Addiction, whether to a substance, activity, or person, is a state of being out of touch with both gratitude and reality. Most of you have heard of "hitting bottom," the moment when you say, "I have a problem that is out of control and it's ruining my life."

What people outside of the twelve-step programs don't usually hear about is "the gratitude cry." At some point, usually during the first year, when the substance or the person is out of your system, you're going to meetings and you've got your sponsor, things are getting better but still aren't good enough. That's how it was for me. I looked at my new life and thought, "Is this all there is?" I was far from satisfied with me or my life. I was afraid that I was never again going to feel joy, or dance till my legs were rubbery, or fall in love. I looked back with horror at how dark and lonely life had been, but also with wistfulness that, sometime way back then, I had felt 'really' alive. But not anymore. Then, something happened.

I heard a voice. Now, I was a practicing psychiatrist at the time. I knew about hallucinations. The only 'normal' hallucination is when you hear your own name called out, clearly or faintly, sometimes in a familiar voice, sometimes not. This is extremely common. Most psychotic hallucinations are like a radio—they're usually as clear and loud and 'sound' as though they're coming from outside your head. People start to talk about voices inside their head when they come to realize that other people don't hear them. There are exceptions, such as those associated with dissociative disorders and dementia, which are qualitatively different, but basically this simple categorization is true.

My voice was different. I heard it as clear as a bell, but as quiet as a heartbeat. It wasn't my own thought; I don't know about you but when I talk to myself, the 'sound' is clearly in my own mind. This voice was neither inside nor outside my head or mind. Rather, this voice felt as though it came from the very center of my body, if that center was also connected by a tiny tunnel deep down into the core of the earth. To put that another way, it came from the furthest part of the universe that still felt like me. It was the "still, small voice" that mystics from all backgrounds have talked about for centuries. I think of it as the voice of God.

You have a right to be skeptical. If you've not experienced this, you may doubt such a thing could happen, or certainly doubt my explanation of it. You might prefer to think it was simply the deepest part of my self addressing me in a crisis. That's fine with me. If, however, you find yourself thinking, "This guy is looney tunes," or even, "This guy can't be a Unitarian," then I challenge you. I'm not looney because this experience affected me deeply in a way that served to make me less crazy.

Trust me: psychotic experiences do not help people, nor heal, nor guide.

I'm also on solid Unitarian Universalist ground because one of our Six Sources is the "direct experience of that transcending mystery and wonder, affirmed in all cultures, which moves us to a renewal of the spirit and an openness to the forces that create and uphold life." It's in the book!

So, to go back to the experience itself, there I was feeling sorry for myself and wondering, "Is this all my life is going to be?" Then came the voice. It didn't say, "I am that I am," as Moses heard in the burning bush, nor did it tell me to build an ark.

It simply said, "Think where you were last year."

And relief—absolute relief—poured in. In fact, my reaction was just as remarkable as the voice itself. It was as though a drop of clear water was put into ink, and the ink became crystal clear. All anxiety, self-pity and doubt simply vanished in an instant. I didn't even have time to think that it was true that a lot had changed for the better that year and would likely keep improving. The knowing of this simply entered my mind and heart instantly.

And then I cried. I cried like an utterly lost child who was just found. I cried like the prodigal son who has discovered there is still a home where love remains. I cried in gratitude. And that gratitude opened me up.

I'd like to say that since then I've lived in gratitude. Back when life was fresh green with recovery, every day held many miracles, and gratitude was easy. Awhile later, I had to remind myself to be grateful, but that would work and I'd feel thankful again. Later still, I began to take it for granted. "Yeah, yeah, I'm grateful for—everything." At times, I realize that I've lost touch with gratitude. There's just too much going on. Work. Meetings. Chores. Just too much.

Holly Bridges Elliott, in her book, *Beholding God in Many Faces*, describes a moment of grace. She's making peanut butter and jelly sandwiches for her children when something makes her stop and just look around. At that moment, she sees the whole room become luminous and "alive with movement," as she puts it. Everything seems to be pulsing and vibrant, like light waves. Joy swells inside her, and she is filled with gratitude. The ordinary is momentarily miraculous, even the water flowing from the tap. Her children suddenly seem to be "eternal beings of infinite singularity and complexity." She knows that one day in the future, she will come to "apprehend [them] in their splendid fullness."

Elliott describes a moment in which utter gratitude breaks through the trance of activity, thought and disconnection in which most of us live through most of our lives. There is just too much to do, to concentrate on, to tire ourselves with; where is the space for a moment of complete perception like hers? Most of the time, we just cannot do it. That is why this is "grace:" an unexpected, unsought and undeserved gift that changes her and the world—she feels called to write it, and we who read it are inspired to see through the mundane. Even if we don't see light waves, we feel gratitude. And if we practice that, then the world is made new.

My gratitude brings me into that new world. It shifts aside questions, doubts and fears, and tells me that, at least for today, I am released. When we live in gratitude, we live with openness to our full heart. In connection with the richness that every day, dreary or brilliant, is steeped with. We live vibrantly. And, practicing gratitude, we will live out our "splendid fullness." We want that. To live with our full heart. Richly. That's living spiritually, isn't it. But, if we think it through, we may have to admit that we don't want that.

If we live completely, embracing each day, we wave a red flag at fate. "Here I am! Open to the moment! Ready for anything!" Be prepared. Just like there's no 'up' without 'down', there is no gratitude without its absence. We've all faced moments of loss or hopelessness, and we will again, but knowing that and opening ourselves to it are two different things. It's not possible to live fully without confronting the abyss. Some of us tumble down into it, afraid for the falling to stop because we fear we won't survive the landing. But, somehow, we do. Others descend on purpose, driven to climb down, deeper and darker because something in there has to be found or retrieved. However we end up on that bottom, we sit in a daze for a moment, an hour, a year. "How can I go on? Is this all there is? What does this mean?"

These are real questions, and the answers must come from a much deeper place than Pollyanna's Glad Game. And that deeper place is found on the bedrock of gratitude.

Last year, I received a call from the first real love of my life, Jean. He was the partner who had treated me best and let me down least. For decades after breaking up, we remained unique friends. His friendship always reminded me that I was lovable every time I forgot. His call was to tell me he had been diagnosed with lung cancer and brain metastases, and it came just as I was finishing the first year of seminary and about to start a chaplaincy internship for the summer. Circumstances made a quick visit very difficult, and Jean insisted that I not come mainly be-cause he had become very anxious and would have been unable not to worry about me if I were nearby. So I neither saw him, nor did I have time to grieve this news.

Jean died just as my second year in seminary was about to begin. The next morning, when I was praying, I found myself thinking how grateful I was for his huge influence in my life and for his enormous love. And feeling this, I finally cried. I cried the grief that I had no space to feel before. I cried in sympathy with his spouse, Daniel, and his large and loving family. But I also cried in gratitude that he brought so much joy and love; that he had died at peace with himself and grateful for his life.

Some people might think that Jean and I were each just playing an adult version of the Glad Game—finding something to be grateful for in the midst of tragedy. I certainly have doubts sometimes when I see people move very quickly from negative feelings towards positive ones. But, I was struck with that connection between grief and gratitude, as though one opened the way for the other. I realized that to acknowledge what is lost and to feel grief is just one step away from seeing what remains and to feel grateful. They go hand in hand.

Unitarian Universalism, in my view, is an absolute commitment to reality. I borrow that phrase from the recovery programs. An absolute commitment to reality. Of course, we debate what reality is. Our blessing is that we don't have to agree on that. But, we tend to agree that we must be committed to it. Our spirituality is largely focused on reality. Our faith defines nothing about any other world, any other plane of existence. Though we are free to believe in things we cannot know in rational, physical terms, our principles do not free us to ignore this world. What happens here is our spiritual concern, our religious commitment. Our blinders must be off and our focus on our hands and feet: what we are doing and where we are. And how we can help make the world better. We strive to see the abyss all around us in this imperfect world and to bridge it, or fill it in, or climb down it with a rope ladder. But, we see it.

If we are committed to seeing the abyss in the world and to doing something about it, we must be committed to seeing it in ourselves and to doing something about it. Glad Games about how well we're doing, how good we are will not carry us far and will not let us be of real use to the world. *But,* it is important to find a Pollyanna spirit within ourselves: that part of us that falls off the roof, grieves and then wakes up to see the whole reality. There are disappointments waiting behind every success. There are blessings all around us hidden in the pain.

At least for today, we can choose to see light waves. To stand in awe that water comes out of a tap. To shine in our splendid fullness. And for that, let us, with eyes wide open and limbs braced for the work, be ever grateful.

Making Peace with a Warring World

Lee Barker, DMin '78 DD '01

Unity Temple UU Congregation

Oak Park, IL

January 2005

It is Election Day in Iraq. I woke this morning and immediately checked on the voting. It is impossible not to be moved by the large numbers of Iraqi citizens who, right this minute, are taking their lives into their hands in order to cast a vote. It is a triumph!

And yet we must be honest about this election.

This is an election in which some candidates are afraid to reveal their identity for fear of being gunned down.

This is an election in which schools doubling as polling places have been closed for a week so that children's lives will not be jeopardized by those who willingly kill the innocent.

This is an election that has a body count associated with it.

This war has been grinding away for two years. I see no end. I am heartsick about it. These are feelings reminiscent of those I carried back in January 1991.

I was minister to another congregation at the time. The previous summer, Iraq had invaded Kuwait and the United States began the huge military ramp-up for the Persian Gulf War. As it intensified, the Unitarian Universalist clergy in my state made a determination to speak out against the impending war. I was pushed forward as our media spokesperson. If optimism had anything to do with it, I was the right choice.

I was optimistic big time. After all, the public was evenly divided over the desirability of that war. It seemed as if the other promoters of peace had a realistic chance of bending the public and the White House toward our religious view: that solutions met through peace have a better prospect of holding than solutions met though war.

There is no surprise ending to the story. It wasn't long into our media campaign that the first bombs were dropped on the people of Iraq. When that happened, my world was pulled away from me. I dropped to the precincts of my own ugly despair, into the bleak place of hopelessness. My fall was prolonged, directly related to my belief that war is humanity's ultimate failure. It is not just the failure of one nation over another, it is not just the failure of one leader over another, and it is not simply the failure of one diplomatic strategy over another. It is the failure of us all. Given that belief, I was confronting my disappointment in all men and women in every time and every place.

I needed help and, in order to gain some contentment in my life, resolved that I would find a way to make peace with this warring world. The real world of war and violence was not going to go away quickly. I had to make my peace with that reality, neither succumbing to it, nor allowing it to smother out my hope that things could be different.

This sermon is for every man and woman who yearns to make a bit of that inner peace for him or herself.

I am not preaching about how you should evaluate this war with Iraq. You may make some assumptions about where I stand and you will probably be exactly right, but that's not my point. My point is that if you are as desperate as I for that contentment with this violent world, you will find it in that person next to you, especially if they disagree with you about this war.

Pam McAllister wrote, "The fabric of the new society will be made of nothing more or less than the threads woven in today's interactions." What she meant by that is that if we are going to paint for ourselves a new, complete world, then we'd better be prepared to put together a reflection of that new complete world, in our lives, in our here-and-now lives. And if we are searching for that new, peaceful world where people of difference are reconciled to one another, despite those differences, then we'd better be prepared to put together a personal world where we are so reconciled to those who are different from us.

And that's why I say to those of you who support this war in Iraq, "In my life you represent humanity's best hope for peace for you are here, in this church, worshipping in a place where you are the distinct minority."

We who come to these liberal churches week after week live out our commitment to hold together even while maintaining our independent beliefs and perspectives. We have created places where each is expected to voice his or her truth, to take one's flame out from under the bushel. In creating this kind of church, we have created a bit of a peace-filled world. That makes these congregations of ours the threads of the new world.

And that, my friends, is reason for hope.

This is not a hope that comes easily. As one friend of mine says, "Anyone can create community with people who believe just like they do. The true test of community rests in the ability to create it with people who disagree with us." And that requires the ability to see the connecting points between oneself and those who outwardly, at least, are our opposites.

One connecting point comes in the understanding that virtually every person, regardless of political stripe, regardless of their stand on this or any other war, takes their stand with the hope of peace. They may believe that war is necessary to get to peace, but it is to peace they wish to go. That's something those who disagree with me, and I, have in common.

We also have in common, something that is far more difficult for me to admit. All of us, me included, have a part of us that is attracted to war.

I'm not sure I could have seen that in myself until I read Chris Hedges' book, *War is a Force that Gives Us Meaning*. Chris Hedges is a foreign correspondent for the New York Times who has covered wars in the Balkans, the Persian Gulf and Central America. Prior to his journalism career, he studied at Harvard Divinity School.

Hedges concludes that, for all of humanity's prayers for peace, for all of the ways we uphold peace as the highest virtue, for all the ways that we mouth peace language, really there is a part of us that hungers for war. There is this part of us that is drawn to it, that looks for excuses for it, that loves the very excitement of it. It is not, he says, simply buying into the myth of glory and patriotism, it is something more. It is also the feeling of exhilaration that comes from being tested in matters of life and death.

Hedges writes extensively of the war in the Balkans in the early and mid-1990s where the landscape was forever scarred by the free-for-all war that raged between people of different religions and ethnicities: Croatian Roman Catholics, Serbian Christian Orthodox and Bosnian Muslims. In a brief period over 200,000 Muslims were savagely killed in genocidal acts, most of them private citizens and many of them women and children. Neighbors, who had previously given one another friendship, inflicted upon one another acts which are simply unspeakable. They forgot the bonds that tied them to one another, forgot so quickly that there was more that connected them than that which separated them.

My wife and I visited my sister in Sarajevo when the war was still a fresh memory there. The city, once so beautiful had a sad and ruined look to it, with its fresh graves filling the public parks, with its war wreckage, the twist of metal and concrete, still standing like monuments to gloom and death. Talking to the people, I got a sense of their sorrow, but I also got a sense of their excitement when they talked about those days. One man, my sister's landlord, talked about how each day that he went to work was a day that he took his life into his own hands, for he had to cross what came to be known as sniper's alley. He would take a long, circuitous route to work each day so that he could have his best chance to dodge those bullets that were aimed in his direction. His eyes sparkled when he spoke about it because when he was so close to death he never felt more alive.

We saw that same expression of sorrow and excitement on the faces of so many there. It is that human tendency not to realize the sanctity of life, not to be able to take a thrill in living until life is threatened.

Here is my confession: I could feel that same tendency in myself. It was exhilarating to be in those places with those people. It made me feel close to death and that granted me the feeling of being wonderfully alive. And I know in my heart it is that same tendency that has led me to peace work over the years. Peace work brings me close to my own mortality and sharpens for me the experience of life.

Maybe we all have these two traits in common. Maybe we all hunger for peace and are sparked to excitement by war. Maybe those are the connecting points that enable us to worship together, form a community with one another, and make some peace with the warring world.

People outside these churches of ours may try to convince us that it is not possible. But I tell them it is. I only have to tell them one true story to make my point.

I turned 18 in 1970. I was draft age during the height of the Vietnam War. I knew that in order to be true to myself that I would seek to be recognized as a conscientious objector, one who opposes war under all circumstances. There was a member of my home Unitarian Universalist congregation who was a Vietnam veteran himself. Jim came back from Vietnam certain that it was right for the United States to be there. We disagreed about everything. He happened to be a teacher in my high school and one day he asked me to stop by his classroom after the final bell. I sat down and he told me he didn't want to be presumptuous, but he was volunteering himself to write a letter to my draft board in which he would vouch for my sincerity. And he said to me, "If you would like, I'll take you to your hearing and wait with you, if you want company."

That's the new world I am hoping for. That's the new world to which I wish to belong. That's a world with which it is possible to find some inner contentment.

It has been 14 years since that first war with Iraq. Maybe it is the fact that it is the second time around that make these days even more difficult than those. The news from Iraq can be heart-stopping. But it doesn't have to defeat our spirits, not if we are willing to act in a manner that is suggested by this great religious tradition of ours. Hope will come to all of those who make a room in our church for persons of each and every opinion. Peace will come to those who open a place in our church for people of every stripe. There is a better way of dealing with human difference. In our church we can both prove it and make some peace with a warring world.

The new world waits. The new world looks a lot like you. It's fabric will be woven in the threads of our own, peace-filled interaction.

Amen

In a Larger Context

Lee P. Page, MDiv '04

Kearsarge Unitarian Universalist Fellowship

Andover, NH

October 2005

It was a cold July day and heavy grey clouds threatened rain. Shivering in her bathing suit, four-year-old Lila stepped gingerly into the shallow swimming area. The young enthusiastic swimming teacher fitted a buoyancy belt with four foam blocks around Lila's waist and Lila, as instructed, obediently lay down in the water and began kicking and paddling.

As her parents and grandparents watched, they were surprised to see her swimming toward the far side of the swimming area. "Wonderful," said the teacher. "Great job; you really don't need all this flotation."

With that the instructor removed one of the blocks and replaced the belt around Lila's waist.

Uh-oh.

Those of us who know Lila realized that the well-meaning swimming instructor had made a critical error. Had she just removed one of the blocks and said nothing, Lila might not have noticed, but she told her what she was doing and that was just enough to tip the balance for Lila from confidence to insecurity and fear of the water.

For the remainder of the lesson, Lila refused to lie down in the water and let her feet float to the surface. Instead she planted her feet firmly on the bottom, leaned over at the waist and paddled with her arms to imitate a swimming motion. No coaxing and no amount of reassurance made any difference. Lila's world had changed and she was now afraid. Had she been older, she might have noticed that the water was very shallow, the instructor was right by her side, and there were three blocks of floatation still on her belt. But what four-year-old has the reasoning ability to see her situation in that larger perspective?

Indeed, who of us has that larger perspective when we feel threatened? Lila's fear reaction is not unique. Each of us responds to physical danger in instinctively programmed ways—either fight, flight, or freeze—-the deer in the head lights reaction. We know that instinctive reaction to danger is a necessary, survival mechanism, but the reliance on fight, flight or freeze as the only ways of dealing with fear does not serve us very well. Secondary thought processes—reason, logic, analysis, planning—are unique to human beings and often are suppressed during a crisis, but they are the resources that will serve us best over time in addressing not only our fear, but the major problems and crises in our lives. Our challenge is to not act or react at just an instinctive level, but to discipline ourselves to engage our higher faculties even as we face our fear.

So today I want to talk a bit about fear and a new fear that we all face. When I say new fear, it is new to Americans, while sadly not new to people in war-torn countries around the world. It is the fear of terrorism. We know from the September 11, 2001 terrorist attack the scale of physical devastation that occurred and the grief and anguish suffered by the people who lost loved ones, or who were caught up in the aftermath. It is not my intent to review the events of that day, but to look at some of the longer-term effects of fear on our lives and on our country.

In his 2004 article, "Resetting the Worry Alarm," Forrest Church says, "Whether sparked by legitimate fright or arising on its own in the mind's creative department, worry is contagious ... I certainly sense that contagion in New York City. ... Orange alert expressed not only an official state of readiness, but also, for many, a personal state of mind."

I don't think that New Yorkers are unique. Fear is gripping our nation and our national leadership. The many speeches we hear in Washington about the war on terrorism reflect that thinking, while they also serve as deliberate attempts to bolster support for the war by exploiting our fears.

Terrorists know that one of their most powerful weapons is to instill so much fear into the national psyche that, in the resulting turmoil and disorganization, the citizens, elected officials and national institutions of power will be unable to function. We don't want to play into terrorist hands by compounding our legitimate anxiety about future attacks with efforts to fan the flames of fear at home.

But any country has somewhat limited options in responding to terrorism. Certainly seeking out and punishing the perpetrators and those who plan or incite violence is of paramount importance, but a nation cannot guarantee security. It cannot "flee" and it cannot "freeze." However, it can "fight." The heightened state of anxiety that has existed in the country since September 11, 2001 has generated such tension that fighting became the option of choice and contributed to the decision to invade Iraq.

How can we best handle our fears both at the personal and national levels so that the irrationality of fear does not control our decision-making? How do we avoid a "fight" response, long enough to harness all the rational, intellectual resources at our disposal? I do have some thoughts about that, but before I respond to that question, I will briefly state the list of things we know not to do.

We know that our instinctive response of fight, flight or freeze is not a good strategy for dealing with long term stress and fear. Acting first and thinking second leads not only to blunders and mistakes, but unanticipated and sometimes tragic long-term consequences.

We also know that going it alone and allowing decisions to be made by just one or a few people can spell disaster. Many minds working together will see the broader implications of actions being considered and will make recommendations often far superior to the choices of only one person.

Another pitfall we know to avoid is to making decisions motivated primarily on emotions, such as hatred or revenge. Acting out of "a tooth for a tooth" or an "eye for an eye" mentality will worsen conditions and will lead only to a world filled with bloodshed and war.

Finally we know that listening to the loudest voice telling us what to do, or following the crowd assuming it must know something we do not, are not necessarily the right choices.

To answer the question of how to make the best decisions during times of insecurity and fear I will tell you about a friend of mine, and what I learned from her.

Nancy and I were in high school and college together. Her husband died in the World Trade Center on September 11, 2001. I had not seen Nancy since her husband's funeral, but this summer I had an opportunity to spend a quiet hour with her. Early in our conversation, she brought up the subject of her husband's death, and she shared openly with me the grief she and her children experienced and her struggle to understand and make sense of his death. I asked her if she had received support and help during this time. She said that she had sought counseling as well as support from her minister. I then asked if she had joined any of the survivor groups that sprang up in her community. She said that she had attended two different support groups, but had stopped going after one meeting.

She described one group as being consumed with hatred not only for the perpetrators of September 11, but for the religion of Islam and Muslim countries in general. The second group was different. They were focused on trying to secure the maximum amount of money from public and private sources to compensate for the loss of present and future income. Neither group, she said, met her needs.

But, with hard work and the support of her counselor and her minister, she was able to gain a greater perspective. She came to believe and to accept that her husband *personally* had not been selected for death, but rather everyone and anyone who happened to be at the targeted sites. She also said that she had come to view his death as bigger than just a personal loss to her, their family and friends, but in a broader context of international relationships between the United States and various countries in the Middle East with complex historical and cultural antecedents. Her husband, she said, had been caught in tragic and complex events of history. Her sadness will remain, but her ability to view her loss in this broader context has helped her accept his death.

What did Nancy teach me? The first thing I learned about her was courage. In the face of grief, fear, and loneliness, she struggled to find answers to her husband death. She did not give in to hatred of all things Islamic, or focus only on money as she knew that these issues, as understandable as they might be, would only lead her away from the understanding she sought, and would emotionally contaminate her life. She did not follow the crowd or retreat into herself to escape. She did not run away or act impulsively in an attempt to avoid sorrow. She stayed in her home and faced the hardship of a life changed forever. She sought professional help and the support of her friends. Her sound approach and hard work paid off.

Nancy's behavior following the death of her husband offer us examples of how to deal more effectively with our fear of terrorism both personally and as a nation. We know that those who commit or support violence must be stopped and punished, but those actions alone are not enough. Nancy knew that she could not retreat into herself or hide or go it alone. We know that as a nation, we cannot retreat and become isolationists. We need to reach out to our allies and promote diplomacy and harmonious international relationships wherever opportunity exists. We must call upon the experience and support of our allies and unite with them in dealing with this international threat. Domestically, all of us, both citizens and elected officials, must have the courage to work smarter. We need to become informed citizens and understand terrorism in the larger context of its origins and the cultures that support it by seeking the advice of Middle East experts. We also must understand and accept responsibility for the roles the United States has played in shaping current and historical events in the Middle East. Americans have been described as "culturally ignorant," and if that is in any way accurate, how can we make intelligent decisions about a part of the world we barely understand? Seeking knowledge and better understanding of these complex issues, as Nancy faced difficult issues in her life, are ways to make better decisions and to control national anxiety. Finally, we must demand from our government a standard of truth, honesty, and transparency in national and international affairs.

As Unitarians Universalists we are challenged to speak up when we disagree with national policy or the actions of our government, even if we are uncomfortable doing so. It is hard to take a stand if one's views are not generally accepted or when one is mocked or labeled as unpatriotic. As Forrest Church stated in the *UU World*, "prudence invites us to be bold, not timid, as long as we aren't foolish." I am happy to see that our denominational leaders and our clergy are being bold by speaking out against fear mongering from Washington, the war in Iraq, the curtailment of civil rights, the rising death toll, and a host of other issues. We have the same opportunity to voice our opinions. The antidote to fear is courage and perseverance, not fight, flight, or freeze.

How do we as Unitarian Universalists reconcile our principles of the inherent worth and dignity of all individuals with those who hate us and wish to destroy our civilization? How do I, how do we, offer justice equity and compassion to those who would never offer them to us? Or how do we feel a part of an interdependent web of existence when there are people for whom that has no meaning? In other words how do we apply our principles to the grimmer reality of life?

My first realization is that our principles will never mirror the reality of current events, because they are the ideals we aspire to and that guide our life. They point in the direction of our highest goals. Secondly, these are the principles that frame the very way of life that terrorism is trying to destroy. Our principles include dignity, worth, justice, responsibility, conscience, democracy, compassion, worthiness, community, peace, liberty, and interdependence. These values are under attack. Now more than ever, we must stay committed to them because they are a source of our strength. So we must face our fears, be guided by our principles, and speak out for what we believe to be true, just and fair.

As a nation we are a model of democracy for the rest of the world. We must insist on honest governance and courageous leaders who will pursue all options for dealing with terrorism rather than just trading violence for violence. The future welfare of the United States and the global community will depend on the actions that we take.

Next summer when the lake warms up, Lila will have more swimming lessons. Will she be able to quell her fears of the water and trust enough to take her feet off the bottom? Only time will tell, but let us hope that by next summer the world will be a bit safer for all the children on earth. May each of us, along with our national leaders, strive to make it so.

Amen

A Moment when
Everything Seems Possible

Karen Stoyanoff, MDiv '96

Prescott, Arizona

July 2005

Last fall I found myself standing in the bushes outside the newborn nursery at Fountain Valley Hospital watching my son and a nurse as my grandson, Luke, had his first introduction to the world. It felt kind of funny standing outside looking in, but that's the procedure at this hospital—there was even a sign on the wall announcing that this was the family viewing area. My youngest son, Jeff, and I stood watching this perfect little new human being with a very healthy set of lungs (we could hear that from outside) and bright blue eyes (that couldn't really see much of anything yet, but still were very alert). His little body was perfect and pink and beautiful.

As I watched him I felt overwhelmed with happiness. Tears formed in my eyes, but they were tears of joy. I tried to understand what it was that was so overwhelming to me in that moment, and suddenly it all came clear.

Looking at Luke right then at the very beginning of his life, I knew that, for him, everything was possible. He could do and be anything that he wanted to, and he was entering a world where the possibilities of what he might experience were unlimited. It was that freedom, that opportunity, that obligation without any limits that was bringing tears of joy to my eyes.

Of course that situation will change as time goes on; choices that he makes or choices that are made for him will begin to set limits on the possibilities open to him. And the world itself will change in ways that set limits for him. And his own body and personality will set limits for him. Sooner, rather than later, he will come to a fork in the road—he will face a choice that means he does one thing and because of what he does, he leaves another behind. The road not taken will set limits for him. As each day passes it will seem like all of those limits become larger and larger. But for that moment, on that magical September evening, there were no limits—everything was possible.

To one extent or another we each have those moments in our lives. Maybe not quite so profound as being present to newborn life, but never-the-less, moments when everything seems possible for us.

I remember it was true for me on the day when my parents drove me to Evanston, Illinois, so I could start college. It seemed like life was starting anew and everything was possible. I could do or be anything I wanted. Maybe for you the feeling came at the start of a new job: on that first day you just knew that the sky was the limit and you could accomplish anything you chose. Or maybe it happened when you began a new relationship, and in the first flush of love, you felt your universe expand until everything seemed possible. In those moments of possibility, there is an unmatchable kind of exhilaration, and a wonderful feeling of personal power. They are moments of pure joy.

But all too soon they end. The world of everyday comes crashing in around us and we face, once again, our own limitations, as well as the limitations imposed upon us by our environment and by our obligations to others. Our world becomes constricted and the possibilities that are open to us shrink down to a precious few, until, like J. Alfred Prufrock, we are once again measuring out our lives in coffee spoons and pondering whether we dare to eat a peach. On our really bad days life may even seem to be reduced to sound and fury, signifying nothing.

But does this need to be true? Is this really the case, or are we opting out of responsible living by so easily accepting the limitations we seem to see—by accepting unquestioningly the constrictions apparently imposed upon us? Do we give up too soon and too easily on the dreams that we have in those moments when everything seems possible? Or maybe even more important: are those moments actually as rare as we seem to think they are? Could it be that every moment is one when everything is possible?

That's what I want to explore with you today, along with the question of what it would take for us to live out the dreams of everything possible in our lives. A friend called me recently and said that she really needed to talk to me. There was an urgency in her voice that prompted me to make a place for her in my schedule. When we met she told me that she was quitting her job—a job in which she was unhappy. I thought about Thoreau and his belief that "most men lead lives of quiet desperation." I always think he was referring to those who stay, quietly, in jobs they hate, or are bored with, or that seem to be stealing their very souls—and they stay because they believe they need to be there in order to survive—because they are convinced that there is nothing else they could do.

But my friend wasn't succumbing to such a fate; she was quitting her unfulfilling job. It's what she told me next, though, that really inspired me. "I'm going to start a program of my own," she said, "something I've always wanted to do." In other words she was going to take a risk and live her dream. And she was telling me not just because I am a friend and she wanted to share this important news with me, but also because she hoped I would be a supporter.

Her plan is a grand one—a big vision—one that might easily fail. It will definitely be difficult to make it happen—to get the financial backing she needs, and the place to house her program, and to find the staff to make it work. But she wasn't letting any of that daunt her. She certainly wasn't letting the fact that it would be easy to simply say, "it's not possible" stop her from working on incarnating her dream. Her enthusiasm was infectious and I was delighted to say I'd be part of her support system.

Then I started wondering, what is it that makes some people see their dreams as guideposts for action instead of as merely wishes too difficult to realize? Tracy Goss, in *The Last Word on Power*, says

> *There are millions of people who genuinely want to make something happen that they, and frequently everyone else, consider impossible. But they feel powerless to do so. It's not that they're incapable. Most of them have already won at the traditional games of life . . . they have leadership positions in large organizations or responsible professional posts. They have comfortable, rewarding, and fulfilling lives. But now they want much more. They want to achieve something meaningful, beyond merely holding an influential position—to start a new sort of organization, redefine the nature of their industry, make government work effectively, right a deeply inbred and prevalent abuse, reshape their workplace, bring a new technology into the world, or simply to be great at what they do. (p. 2)*

So, again, I ask, why is it that some people are willing to live their dreams and others not? Goss goes on to say,

> *The most capable, legendary, inspiring leaders we know of have one thing in common. They have made the impossible happen. ... Wilbur and Orville Wright developed the power to fulfill a dream as old as the human species. Mahatma Gandhi called forth the power to compel the British to walk out of India. Rosa Parks, in refusing to give her seat to a white man, did not merely spark a revolutionary alteration in racial attitudes, she embodied a powerful stand that forced an entire country to take notice. Betty Friedan reframed the mainstream American culture's attitude toward women; Betty Ford re-*

framed its attitude toward addiction. (p. 8)

I'm sure we could come up with a great laundry list of reasons why these people and countless others have dared to live their dreams, but that's not as important as asking, what's holding the rest of us back?

I can't answer that question for you. I don't think it's even appropriate for me to try to answer that question for you and I know it's not important for me to answer that question for anyone but myself. What I do think is essential to this message is that I ask the question and urge you to spend time thinking about it for yourself.

Let me repeat: what's holding you and me back from making our dreams a reality? I'll put it another way—what would you dare to dream if you knew you couldn't fail? As I wrote those words I remembered that Susan B. Anthony, in her last address to suffragettes, almost 100 years ago, said, "Failure is impossible." I believe she also meant that failure was unthinkable—therefore it must be rendered impossible. What is so important in your life that you would say of it, "failure is impossible"? And what are you doing to make that dream or goal a reality in your life.

If I go back to the list of people I mentioned earlier who lived their dreams into reality, I notice that the common denominator for each of them seems to be that they were passionate about those dreams. So I would ask you, what are you passionate about and how are you making that part of your life?

Earlier I mentioned the obligations we have to others or to our society as a whole. We can easily let these two things become restrictions in our lives—restrictions that stop us from taking a risk and doing what we most dearly want to do. But do we have to give up our dreams because of our obligations? What if Susan B. Anthony and Mahatma Gandhi had taken this route instead of living their dreams?

Certainly there must be a balance between what we must do for the others in our lives and what we must do not just for ourselves, but for the dreams we have of a better world. If we do not strike that balance we may soon find ourselves back to the dilemma of a life of quiet desperation. And then who is benefiting from our sacrifice? I would suggest that no one is. And I know I've been giving you only examples of famous people who took risks or did something that seemed extraordinary, but that's because those are the examples we can all recognize.

We have much smaller examples in our own lives all the time. I remember how unhappy I was when my children were small and I was a stay-at-home mom. I loved my kids dearly, but I felt like I was wasting my talents and my life by staying out of the workforce. I lived in a community where my attitude was considered negligence and knew that if I went back to work I would suffer censure. And not a little dose of guilt, as well! And for a while I lived with that sense of obligation overwhelming my dreams. But finally it became too difficult—I knew that I had to do something beyond childcare and I went back to work part-time.

I'd love to tell you that no one ever said anything to me that was critical, but I can't. I certainly heard about what a bad mother I was— my uncle even asked me why I had children if I didn't want to stay home and take care of them. But, despite all those comments, what was immediately evident to my husband and me was that I was a much better parent when I felt better about myself and my life—when I refused to simply plod along in quiet desperation.

Now it's obvious to me that the key to all of this is balance. There are obligations that we have to those around us—there are people who are counting on us. But there is also another obligation to a world in need, to a hurting society, and to ourselves. I know that the tears I felt upon seeing all the possibilities in the new life of my grandson were prompted in part by how hard it is to stay with the dream of what might be possible and how much easier it is to focus on the limitations that are keeping us locked in the status quo. In her book, *Rock of Ages at the Taj Mahal*, Meg Barnhouse, a Unitarian Universalist minister, talks about not wanting to waste her life. I don't want to end my life saying I wasted it and I don't imagine you do either. Meg has come up with wonderful dreams for making life worthwhile; they are so very ordinary and yet immeasurably precious. She wants to raise her children with honesty and love. What parent could argue with that? She wants to make music and see beauty, and both of those things are available to us if we will just stop and pay attention. The next one is a little more difficult: she wants to get along with her relatives. But the truth is that most of the time that too is possible, if we are just willing to work at it. And when it's not possible, it is rarely with all our relatives, only with a select few. And then she says she'd like to make a soul connection with her friends, and I take that to mean that she wants a deep and intimate relationship with those she calls friends—again something that is possible with a little work. The next one is also hard—or at least a little riskier. She wants to claim her right to tell the truth as she sees it. It's certainly something we can all do, it just doesn't always work out as comfortably as we might like. What I'm struck by with all of these items is that they are dreams for a life well lived, but they aren't world shaking. They are actually quite personal and the sort of things that no one except her close companions would know about. Every single one of them is immanently doable. What they take is focus. What they take is intentionality.

That's what I've really been talking about today. We all have dreams—I don't have to tell you to have dreams about what you would like life to be like. But if we allow ourselves to be trapped by perceived limitations or we fall prey to the overwhelming minutiae of our daily existence, it is easy to let those dreams die without ever trying to incarnate them. Erma Bombeck wrote a lovely essay on dying in which she said she wished she'd spent less time dusting. Of course I don't know whether you want to take her word for anything since she also said, "Anyone who watches three football games in a row should be declared brain dead." Perhaps more to the point would be that she said, "There are people who put their dreams in a little box and say, 'Yes, I've got dreams, of course I've got dreams.' Then they put the box away and bring it out once in awhile to look in it, and yep, they're still there." If we do that, if we don't even think about those dreams except on special occasions like the birth of a child, then we run the serious risk of keeping them in a box where they will ultimately dry up and die. And that would be a travesty, a negation of the importance of our lives.

I left out one of Meg's dreams. She also said, "Oh, and I want to be wonderful." And don't we all! But what does that mean, 'be wonderful'? How will we know if we've succeeded? There are probably as many recipes for wonderful as there are people to think about it. So, again, I'm going to encourage you to think that one through for yourselves. It's not particularly important what I say about it, but it is important that you spend some time deciding for yourself what it might be.

To tickle your thinking cap I'll go back to Erma Bombeck one more time, and tell you that she said, "When I stand before God at the end of my life, I would hope that I would not have a single bit of talent left and could say, 'I used everything you gave me.'" That reminds me of that George Bernard Shaw quote where he says "I want to be thoroughly used up when I die." We hear that part of the quote often, but listen to what comes just before it:

> *This is the true joy in life, the being recognized by yourself as a mighty one; the being thoroughly worn out before you are thrown on the scrap heap; the being a force of nature instead of a feverish selfish little clod of ailments and grievances complaining that the world will not devote itself to making you happy.*

For me, this would be a good place to start on deciding what I might mean if I asked to be considered wonderful!

Whatever you decide, we need dreamers to make this world a better place. And whatever you decide you are entitled to a dream and to believe that it is possible. I believe that every moment can be a moment when everything is possible if we are just willing to dream. I'm going to close today with some words from Lawrence of Arabia, who said,

> *Those who dream by night in the dusty recesses of their minds wake in the day to find that all was vanity;*

> *But the dreamers of the day are dangerous people, for they may act their dream with open eyes, and make it possible.*

LONG COME THE MILLENNIUM

Mark Ward, MDiv '04

Unitarian Universalist Church of Asheville, NC

May 2005

There it sits at the end of the Christian Bible like some monstrous exclamation point. The Revelation to John: a document purporting to be a letter from a persecuted, late first-century Christian prophet unveiling the contents of his vision of how Jesus would return to Earth, punish the wicked, redeem the saved and inaugurate a celestial kingdom of God for the rest of all time.

For the casual reader of the Bible, stumbling into the Book of Revelation can come as a shock. It is like nothing else in the New Testament: full of wave after wave of violent imagery, with bizarre persons and fantastical animals shifting shapes like something out of a nightmare, and a picture of Jesus more nearly approaching Attila the Hun than the gentle shepherd of the gospels.

To this day Revelation remains the most controversial book of the Bible. It almost didn't make it into the canon of the Bible to begin with, and, when Protestant reformers in the 16th and 17th centuries reappraised the Bible, some sought to throw it out. But as bizarre as it is, Revelation has always seemed to find a following, especially among those feeling marginalized or dispossessed. That is, after all, the position that the book's self-identified author, John of Patmos, claims for himself. Introducing his vision, John cites the oppression of early Christian communities by the Roman Empire and makes clear that the ultimate message behind all the fantastical imagery is that his oppressors will get their comeuppance, and soon.

I must tell you that I am no fan of the Book of Revelation, for reasons I will explore in more detail later. But given the increasing prominence it and its prophesies are playing in increasingly public debates, I think it's wise for us to have at least a nodding familiarity with it, and so let me offer this brief sketch.

The story begins with an image of Jesus consoling and criticizing seven churches in Asia Minor, warning of the end times to come. Then opens a vision of a celestial throne room where God presides, holding a scroll in his hand. At his right side is a lamb, representing Jesus, who, as he opens the scroll's seven seals, unveils the trials and torments to come. The opening of the seventh seal brings a series of seven trumpet blasts, announcing the coming of one catastrophe after another: the seas turned to blood, the rivers bitter poison, the darkening of the sun and the stars, and so on.

Before the catastrophes, though, John is assured that an army of 144,000 elect (representing 12,000 from each of the 12 tribes of Israel), will avoid the tribulation and join Jesus in the upcoming battle to defeat the forces of evil. Other believers, he is told, will have to endure the trials, but can expect a home in the heavenly city in the end.

The cycles of seven continue with seven visions of the days to come, and seven bowls representing specific plagues God sends down. Here is where we hear about the coming of the antichrist, who will attempt to delude believers, and his false prophets, as well as the arrival of two beasts, one from the sea and one from the land—marked by the number 666—all of whom bring havoc to the Earth until the arrival of an army of angels, who defeat them.

John is assured that Christ is then to preside over a thousand-year reign. But the devil is not done yet. He reappears and attempts again to deceive the nations. In the end, however, fire rains down from the heavens and destroys the infernal forces. At this point, the final judgment occurs: the saved are raised to dwell in a heavenly city, a new Jerusalem of eternal joy and bliss. The rest are cast with Satan into a lake of fire and obliterated.

As foreign as all this appears to us today, it would not have seemed so at the time it was written. Biblical scholars point out that the images John uses are not unique to Revelation. They are, instead, a pastiche of language from Jewish epiphany stories, such as the Book of Daniel, as well as Greek myths and other stories told by other Middle Eastern cultures.

Revelation is, in fact, part of a vast genre of apocalypses that were told at the time. Why the sudden popularity of this style? It's been suggested that part of the reason may be that the area was a crossroads occupied by many cultures that often came into conflict. Even more was the impact of the Roman Army. Rome at the time had been struggling to hold its empire together, and pesky religious cults that refused to observe the state religion were dealt with harshly.

From all appearances it is Rome that John had in mind when he wrote of a 10-horned beast from the sea that ruled the world and demanded worship, as well as the whore of Babylon who sits on seven mountains. It also appears that the number 666, identified as the mark of the beast, is meant to symbolize the Roman Emperor Nero, who was particularly merciless in the persecution of Christians.

It is possible, then, to explain the Book of Revelation, as some Christians do, as a historic document: one that describes the troubles of the church as a particular point in time. One could argue, in the words of scholar Marcus Borg, that in reading Revelation we should attend, not so much to its florid images, but to its larger message: a warning against "domination systems organized around power, wealth, seduction, intimidation and violence," that we recognize them as antithetical to the true teachings of Jesus. We could have a civilized discussion around this topic. And that would be fine.

What troubles me is those who read the horrors of Revelation a different way. Paul Boyer, in his book, *When Time Shall Be No More*, points out that the images of Revelation and the drama of the battle in the last days have been woven through church writings and teachings for centuries. Part of what motivated the Crusades, for example, was a belief that driving off Muslims would prepare the way for the new Jerusalem.

During the Protestant Reformation, as familiarity with the Bible spread, imagery from Revelation found wider use. Leaders who were disliked were vilified as the antichrist: the Pope was a common target of this charge, or Turkish leaders of the Ottoman Empire, or whatever king, or bishop was out of favor. Our own Puritan ancestors seeking to make a "new Jerusalem" in North America made strong use of the imagery of Revelation. Preachers speculated about whether America, rather than the Middle East, might be the true seat of the new heavenly city.

It was the Great Awakening in the middle of the 18th century that saw an explosion of millennial expectation. Jonathan Edwards, especially, laid the groundwork for looking to the Book of Revelation to explain current events. Some even sought to explain the American Revolution in apocalyptic terms.

The Great Awakening later lost its tug on the established churches—the rise of Unitarianism at the time may have even had something to do with that—but not on the popular imagination. With the coming of the 19th century, established preachers and intellectual leaders pretty much abandoned the project of interpreting current events in terms of scripture.

In their place arose a new generation of evangelicals who took on the task. Unlike many of their predecessors, though, these were skeptical of any hope for earthly reform. They set their sights, instead, on divine intervention. Perhaps the most famous of these was William Miller, a Baptist layman and farmer who calculated the date of the apocalypse at October 22, 1884. The passing of that date disappointed the Millerites, but didn't discourage the project of millennial expectation. Miller's followers, in fact, were among those who continued the work and later established the Seventh Day Adventist church.

One especially influential minister, John Darby, a Scotch Presbyterian, in the 1850s calculated a series of what he called "dispensations" that God had laid down. The current cycle, he claimed, ended with Jesus' crucifixion. The next would begin with what he called "the Rapture," the moment when believers would rise to meet Christ in the air.

The popularity of this apocalyptic perspective has risen and fallen over the years, with different writers adding their own spins and elaborations. But in many respects it has remained the same: the rapture awaits those who are true to the faith. The only question remaining is, when? As wars, earthquakes, epidemics and the like come and go, the timing changes. As a rule, the answer remains, as it was with John of Patmos, soon.

If you are curious to find out—from the evangelical perspective— just how soon, I invite you to Google the rapture index on the worldwide web. Compilers of the index track 45 trends that they consider indicators of the rapture's coming, from Satanism, to the economy, to wild weather. You may be interested to know that they consider the threat of "liberalism" right now to be pretty low. Eighty-five on the index is low; up to 145 is high. For anything higher, the category is, "Fasten your seat belts."

The current rating is 150.

Now, as I said, I am no fan of the Book of Revelation. As a historical artifact I suppose it holds some interest, but as any kind of guide to faith I can find no use for it. But, then again, I'm a pluralist when it comes to religion. Different strokes for different folks, right? If people want to spend their time combing over Revelation and computing the timing of the last days, that's their business. And I say that knowing that those particular folks, as a rule, are not pluralists. They are convinced of the truth of their belief and feel certain that when the day they await arrives, I will be among those cast into the lake of fire. That's a chance I'm willing to take.

What worries me far more is the rise recently of a new movement among evangelicals that not only awaits the rapture, but is determined to garner the political power to begin what they see as God's work, the imposition of their notion of a Christian nation.

In the May 2005 issue of *Harper's*, author Chris Hedges tells of visiting a Christian Broadcasters conference where he learns of a new movement among evangelicals called "dominionism." The group's goal, he learns, is to bring America under what it calls "Christian dominion." Under this vision, the nation would be governed essentially by the 10 commandments, education would be based on Creationism and what are called "Christian values," the federal government's role would be limited to protecting property rights and "homeland security," churches would run social welfare agencies, and the death penalty would be imposed for a host of "moral crimes," ranging from blasphemy to sodomy and witchcraft.

Not all evangelicals there were signed on to this radical agenda, Hedges wrote, but the support for it appeared to be growing. This is a shift from years ago, when evangelicals distanced themselves from the larger society and disdained politics as craven and corrupt. In the last couple of decades, though, they have entered politics in a big way, strongly influencing elections at every level across the country, to the point where today politicians from President George Bush and the leaders of Congress on down either identify themselves as evangelical or are sympathetic to the evangelical perspective.

But here I think I should stop and make something clear. It is not so much the strictly religious element of this perspective that is disturbing me as it is something deeper. There is a fundamental way of viewing the world that underlies what I am calling the evangelical perspective. It sees the world in blacks and whites, missing the nuances.

George Lakos in his book *Moral Politics* describes it as a view that sees the world as basically dangerous, where strength and authority are of primary importance. There is one moral path—the straight and narrow—and each person is expected to stick to it. Rules are firm and unbendable, delivered, again, by those in authority, and maintained through personal discipline.

In his *Harper's* article, Hedges says that as he was leaving the broadcasters conference he recalled words he heard 25 years ago from his ethics professor at Harvard—Unitarian Universalist theologian James Luther Adams. Adams was in his eighties at the time and told the students that watching the rise of Pat Robertson and other evangelicals speaking of their ambition to take control of American institutions reminded him of his experience visiting Nazi Germany in the 1930s. Hedges said Adams warned the students, then in their 20s, that when they reached his age they would all be fighting what he called "Christian fascists."

The ideological inheritors of that brutal political movement of the 1930s would return, he said, not wearing swastikas or brown shirts, but would cloak themselves in the language of the Bible, carrying crosses and chanting the Pledge of Allegiance.

Adams reminded the students that in the 1930s many religious liberals failed to understand the power and allure of such "evil," and he feared that when the radical Christians came pushing their agenda, these good people "would undoubtedly play by the old, polite rules of democracy, long after those in power had begun to dismantle the democratic state." Adams, Hedges said, "knew how desperately people want to believe the comfortable lies told by totalitarian movements, how easily those lies lull moderates into passivity."

Now, I want to be clear that it is not my practice to demonize others or condemn those with whom I disagree with inflammatory words. I believe in building—not blowing up—bridges, working through differences and looking for common ground.

And yet, I'm hearing Jim Adams' words echoing in my mind. The truth is the nightmarish world he described is one I see unfolding before my eyes: a Christian right, vying not just for followers, but for dominion. And I find myself asking, am I just another one of those polite religious liberals, playing by the old rules while I watch the democratic state being dismantled? Isn't it time we put down our marker and made our stand?

In the May 15, 2005, *New York Times Book Review*, Mark Lilla notes that from America's founding the role of religion has been complex. While on one hand the founders sought to keep the church and state separate, they also hoped that religion could assist the state by helping to form good citizens. Their hope, he said, was essentially two-fold: that, if they were guaranteed liberty, "religious sects would grow attached to liberal democracy and obey its norms," and that by entering the public square, religions would become less dogmatic and more rational.

In fact, religions in America pretty much did follow that path until the 1960s or so when most of the mainline faiths went into decline in the face of evangelical, Pentecostal and other charismatic faiths.

The problem of the liberal approach to religion, he said, is that it "imagines a pacified order in which good citizenship, good morals and rational belief coexist harmoniously. It is therefore unprepared when the messianic and eschatological forces of biblical faith begin to stir."

We live today in a time when messianic forces are more than stirring. They are hard at work trying to reshape the fabric of this nation and religion's place in it. And impelling that work, is a view organized around not the give-and-take of representative democracy, but a fearful and oppressive vision of apocalyptic horror and death.

Never has it been more important that we who see the world otherwise appreciate, in Jim Adams' words, the power and allure of that viewpoint. It is not crazy or delusional or anything like that. It is calculating, organized and influential. To counter it, and I think we must counter it, we, too, must organize, strategize and prepare ourselves to respond.

We must be prepared to make the case for freedom, reason and tolerance, for the worth and dignity of every person, for the right of conscience and the spirit's call arising from within each of us, for understanding our lives as centered on this good earth, interwoven with all existence.

In the meantime, we must also be willing to engage others, not only in debate but also in loving concern, to affirm their humanity and their dignity when others would not.

One Unitarian Universalist minister I know tells the story of running into a former neighbor who had been a fundamentalist but had left the church. This minister had been struggling with the question of what religious liberals could say to help those with fundamentalist beliefs consider a different viewpoint.

After listening to the woman's story of leaving the church, the minister asked the woman if she thought there was anything that she, the minister, could have done or said to encourage the woman to ask the questions that ultimately led to her leaving the church. The woman thought for a long time and then said, "No, not really, because anything you would have said would have been corrupt." But, she said, "your kindness to me and comfort with your own path to salvation is one of the things that started me wondering, what if they're wrong?"

It is critical that, as we work to organize a response in support of our life-affirming faith—one that sees salvation as the work for wholeness and reconciliation of all humankind—we also stay true to our principles and our own humanity.

Let our work be grounded in the love and hope that are at the center of our movement. Let us dedicate ourselves to the path of ever unfolding possibility. Let us give thanks, for a universe that fills us with awe and challenges our imaginations, for this fragile earth and the joy of human life, for the oneness of human community transcending all separation, for high hopes and noble causes and faith without fanaticism, for those who labor for a fairer world, for opportunities to change and grow, affirm and choose, that we may live not by our fears but by our hopes.

And in the words of one of our hymns, may nothing evil cross this door. May peace walk softly through these rooms. And, though these sheltering walls are thin, may they be strong to keep hate out and hold love in.

So be it.

BIBLIOGRAPHY

Anand, Mulk Raj. *Untouchable.* New York: Penguin Books; Reprint Edition, 1990.

Barnhouse, Meg. *Rock of Ages at the Taj Mahal.* Skinner House Books, 1998.

Boyer, Paul. *When Time Shall Be No More.* Harvard University Press, 1992.

Brussat, Frederic & Mary Ann. *Spiritual Literacy: Reading the Sacred in Everyday Life.* Scribner, 1998.

Buehrens, John A. and Forrest Church. *A Chosen Faith: An Introduction to Unitarian Universalism,* rev. ed. Boston: Beacon Press, 1998: 119.

Church, Forrest. "Resetting the Worry Alarm." *UU World,* October 2004: 31.

Elliott, Holly Bridges. *Beholding God in Many Faces.* Saint Mary's Press, 1993.

Gervais, M.D., Robert P. "The Necessity of Free-Market Prices for Medical Care." *Journal of Physicians & Surgeons.* V9.2 (Summer, 2004).

Goss, Tracy. *The Last Word on Power.* New York: Doubleday, 1995.

Hedges, Chris, "Soldiers of Christ II." *Harpers Magazine.* May 2005: 55-61.

———. *War is a Force that Gives Us Meaning.* Anchor Books, 2003.

Bibliography

Lakos, George. *Moral Politics.* University of Chicago, 2002.

Lilla, Mark. *New York Times Book Review.* May 15, 2005: 39.

McCullough, David. *John Adams.* Simon & Schuster, 2001.

Medwin, Michelle. *Press & Sun Bulletin.* April 23, 2005: 5B.

Rubin, Bonnie Miller. "Medical bills pave way to poor house." *Chicago Tribune.* Feb 2, 2005.

Sacks, Jonathan. *The Dignity of Difference.* Continuum International Publishing Group, second ed., 2003: 60.

About the Authors

Valerie Mapstone Ackerman, MDiv '98, practices peace-making ministry in rural and urban Oklahoma. Her work includes chaplaincy in a multidisciplinary domestic violence intervention program, itinerant preaching and teaching, organizing for sustainability and justice, and building community capacity for non-violence as the director of Peace House in Tulsa, Oklahoma.

Stephen Atkinson is a retired psychiatrist from Fredericton, New Brunswick, in Canada. Prior to seminary, he won awards for short fiction and drama writing.

Lee Barker, DMin '78 DD '01, has served as president of Meadville Lombard Theological School since 2003. Before coming to Meadville Lombard, his 25 years of parish ministry were noted for his leadership in interfaith, peace and justice efforts.

David E. Bumbaugh, BD '64, Minister Emeritus of the Unitarian Church in Summit, New Jersey, is Professor of Ministry at Meadville Lombard Theological School. He is the author of *The Education of God* and *Unitarian Universalism: A Narrative History*, and chapters in *A Language of Reverence*, *Narnia Revisited*, *A Bold Experiment*, and *Experiencing Poverty*.

John A. Cullinan is in his final year of studies at Meadville Lombard and is a member of the First Unitarian Society of Milwaukee. He served as intern minister and summer minister for the 2005-2006 church year at Unity Temple Unitarian Universalist Congregation in Oak Park, Illinois.

Edward Frost, DMin '74, is Senior Minister Emeritus of The Unitarian Universalist Congregation of Atlanta, Georgia. He has produced two books, *With Purpose and Principle*, a history of the development of the

Unitarian Universalist Principles and Purposes, and *Coming Alive*, a book of sermons. He is a winner of the 2004 Borden Prize for sermon writing.

Patrick T. O'Neill, DMin '79, has been a parish minister for twenty-seven years serving UU congregations in Washington, Massachusetts, and Delaware. He was the 2005 Preacher of the Living Tradition at the Unitarian Universalist Association General Assembly.

Aaron McEmrys is a second-year student at Meadville Lombard Theological School, where he is preparing for ministry. Before coming to Meadville Lombard, Aaron worked as a union organizer and educator. He received his Bachelor of Arts from the National Labor College at the George Meany Center for Labor Studies.

Lee Page, MDiv '04, is a community minister who works as a hospice chaplain and pastoral care counselor.

Karen Stoyanoff, MDiv '96, serves as the minister of Orange Coast Unitarian Universalist Church in Costa Mesa, California. Before becoming a Unitarian Universalist minister, she spent 30 years in the field of education and training. She is currently active in community and social action groups in California and has most recently completed a term as Minister in Residence at Meadville Lombard Theological School. She is also a member of the Board of Trustees of Meadville Lombard.

Douglas Taylor, MDiv '99, is minister of the Unitarian Universalist Congregation of Binghamton, New York. He is author of two meditations in the Meditation Anthology, *For All That Is Our Life*, and has an impressive collection of colorful and crazy socks.

Matt Tittle, MDiv '04, is Minister of the Bay Area Unitarian Universalist Church in Houston, Texas. He is a retired naval officer, former university professor, and author of *Taking Back Faith: Heretical Thoughts* *for a New Century.*

Mark Ward, MDiv '04, is minister of the Unitarian Universalist Church of Asheville, North Carolina. Before entering the ministry, he had a 25-year career in newspaper journalism in Milwaukee, Wisconsin and Charleston, West Virginia.

About Meadville Lombard

Meadville Lombard Theological School is a Unitarian Universalist seminary providing a graduate education grounded in our faith tradition. We offer three degree programs plus lifelong learning opportunities for all who seek to take the next great leap forward on their spiritual journey.

Our degree programs include:

- A four-year Master of Divinity for those seeking ordination;
- A two-year Master of Arts in Religion for those seeking to become who they are called to be (such as a lay leader in a congregation, a certified religious educator, or a public servant fully engaged in proclaiming Unitarian Universalist values to the world);
- A self-paced Doctor of Ministry for those with three or more years service in ministry.

Situated in the Hyde Park neighborhood of Chicago, we are affiliated with the University of Chicago and the Association of Chicago Theological Schools, whose ten independent seminaries make this city such a rich learning environment.

Our Mission

We educate students in the Unitarian Universalist tradition to embody liberal religious ministry in UU congregations and wherever else they are called to serve. We do this in order to take into the world our Unitarian Universalist vision of justice, equity, and compassion.

Visit our website at
www.meadville.edu